Too Much Too Young?

Susie Fisher was born in 1949. She took a degree in psychology and philosophy at Oxford and went on to Harvard to do a further degree in clinical psychology. She is married and lives in London, where together with Susan Holder she runs a market research company called Youth Profile.

Susan Holder was born in 1949. She trained as a teacher and then worked for the ILEA and the Department of Employment before moving to an advertising agency and starting a career in research.

Susie Fisher and Susan Holder

Too Much Too Young?

Pan Original
Pan Books London and Sydney

Dedication
To the kids

Acknowledgements
With thanks to Denise Davies at Youth Profile who nursed us through and kept everything running smoothly; the Schlackman Group and in particular Wendy Gordon who started the lifestage project, and Bill Schlackman for his infamous support; Neale Pharoah, Lisa Hampton, Jeff Chambers and Dee Rivaz who helped us with the original data; John Nicholson who showed us the way; Fearless Fred; and finally Michael Dempsey who cajoled this book out of us, and gave us the courage to write it at all.

First published 1981 by Pan Books Ltd,
Cavaye Place, London SW10 9PG
© Susie Fisher and Susan Holder 1981
ISBN 0 330 26480 X
Set in Great Britain by
Northumberland Press Ltd, Gateshead, Tyne and Wear
Printed and bound by
Richard Clay (The Chaucer Press) Ltd, Bungay, Suffolk

Contents

1 Opening up

Simon, Kevin and Robert edge in through the door; they have been hanging about on the street too embarrassed to come in on their own. They lodge themselves uncomfortably in chairs around the room and avoid my eyes.

All are dressed alike in jeans, shirt and dark sweater and not one will part with his combat jacket, even though it is much too hot. They all have neat short haircuts. Robert is wearing big flamboyant boots, with pointed toes and Cuban heels.

Mark joins us, grabs *Mad* magazine off the floor and buries himself behind it. Silence.

Gerald arrives and nervously gabbles at the others, who ignore him. Finally, very late, Andy swaggers in, fingering the chain round his neck, throws himself down on the remaining chair and pretends he is too manly to mind the embarrassing squeak it makes every time he moves. We are complete.

The first thing which strikes me is that even though they are all 14 or 15 they are different sizes. Mark is a young man with a five o'clock shadow and Robert is a big child with silky hair and a downy complexion. Kevin is small and tougher than all of them.

I feel reassured now they are all in front of me. They are tough all right, but they don't seem alien, so I break the silence and explain the point of the group. Nobody speaks. You can sense them thinking, 'It's a con.' Now what do I do? Finally, Andy, who is to emerge as spokesman, asks, 'What do you want us to say?' I remember my checklist. 'Tell me what schools you go to,' I say – and we are away. Cautiously, they try out remarks about the subjects they are taking and the exams they are studying for. This is obviously the edited version for adults – it sounds suspiciously 'goody-goody'. But soon Kevin is complaining about the rotten teaching, Simon is describing how he and his mates got the teacher back by drop-

1

ping crisp packets on him from a great height and Andy is painting a vivid picture of his history teacher leaning over his desk in her low-cut blouse.

Once they realize I am not there to criticize, they have no trouble talking, they start bragging and sizing one another up. The conversation veers on to fights. This is worth talking about. Move by move they savour the fight in the last episode of *The Sweeney*. With gusto they relive the gang fights in the neighbourhood and their own hair-raising exploits on the streets. The sandwiches arrive and are demolished instantly. We talk about television, fashion, cults, how to score with your girlfriend, how many times you've been drunk. I go out and come back to find they had been recording rude remarks on my tape recorder and have nicked half my supplies of shandy. They enjoy my discomfiture.

After eyeing me up, they decide to trust me and ask if they can smoke. I begin to understand the agony of having to hand round a packet of fags which costs you a quarter of your week's income.

As they leave, they threaten not to come back next week – but as it happens they all get there early instead. They are wearing their best clothes. It is Robert's birthday. I am touched and very pleased to see them.

This is a quieter session. Having decided to trust me and each other, they are ready to drop some of the bravado. We talk about how much Mum means to them, but how sometimes you have to lie to her; how Dad is never there; how they worry about exams and the future. They pester Mark to tell them what shaving is like; they listen with awe as Andy talks about having sex with his bird. They admit that it's a problem having to prove you're a man, when you look about eleven, and how scared they are of asking a girl for a date.

They are drawing support from their common experience. Four hours is a long time to sit still and talk, when what you like doing best is roaming the streets. But they enjoy being forced to think about themselves and are eager for me to ask questions. Their energy and aggression is channelled into the present, for they don't often look at themselves in perspective.

I feel they are grateful that an adult is showing enough interest to ask, and they boost my ego in return by asking what I am doing after the group.

They and I are reluctant to bring the group to a close, but Kevin's Dad is coming to collect him at nine, so we have to. They tell me gruffly that if I need any more information, I can come back to them. I watch them wind down the road on their bikes, feeling a great liking for all of them.

The project

That was the first of eight discussion groups with teenagers, and the first part of a nationwide study of teenagers which was started in March 1980.

You might be wondering who we are, and what our interest is in listening to teenagers. You might be wondering if we have a vested interest and who pays us to do it anyway? Well, we are not youth leaders, civil servants or members of the Salvation Army. We are market researchers, Susie Fisher and Susan Holder. We are conducting the study on behalf of a mixed bag of people – retailers, financial institutions and manufacturers – who believe, like us, that if you are going to design goods and services for kids then you ought to understand something more about their lives than whether or not they like Coca-Cola. Our research company specializes in work with kids so we were keen to do a basic study to see how they view their own lives. We wanted to understand their priorities, and we did not want to avoid issues such as money, shops, advertising and television, which tend to get left out of other surveys. The media love to sensationalize youth, the papers are full of horror stories about sex and illiteracy, vandalism and violence. We wanted to put these images behind us and go out and talk to the mainstream – the sons and daughters of all the people who go to work every day, shop at the supermarket and like to watch television in the evenings. People like us and people like you.

We decided that kids change a lot during their teens, so it didn't make sense to try to cover every one or we'd have ended up with a superficial impression. We wanted the time to listen to the kids in detail, so we chose to talk only to teenagers who

3

were at secondary school, that is from the age of eleven up to sixteen. This gave us a chance to see how they change as they approach puberty and how they develop afterwards, but stopped short of following them into jobs and further education.

We were lucky, because the market research profession was already set up to recruit whoever we wanted to talk to. Behind every little office in London is a nationwide network of ladies of all ages and from all walks of life, who acted as agents to help us find exactly the kind of people we needed to interview.

If we had happened to need a group of women who take holidays in the South of France, dye their hair green and have birthdays in November, a good recruiter would have found them for us somehow! She might knock on doors, stand in the street, question her daughter's school friends or raid the WI. She would know the resources of her own neighbourhood better than we could.

For this survey, though, there were almost no restrictions. We wanted to talk to kids in general, across the country. We asked the recruiters to find us particular age groups and were careful to divide our sample equally between middle-class and working-class families. This was determined by a standard classification which depends on the occupation of the head of the household. Each recruiter was assigned either a group of boys or a group of girls and was asked to get as wide a range as possible, avoiding obvious biases such as recruiting them all from the local football team.

In the first part of the study we ended up with eight groups – 11–12-year-old girls from Windsor, 13–14-year-old girls from Culcheth in Lancashire, 14–15-year-old girls from Sheffield, 15–16-year-old girls from Roehampton. The boys were 11–12-year-olds from Manchester, 13–14-year-olds from Dagenham, 14–15-year-olds from Kilburn in London, and 15–16-year-olds from Leeds. Seventy-six per cent of the UK population lives in cities, and this survey is more a picture of urban than rural teenagers.

Putting kids together in groups their own age was a good way to get them to talk. Most of them were at different schools so

4

they didn't know each other to begin with. They had to draw on common experiences to get into conversation. Some issues were difficult to talk about in a group, so we talked to another twelve teenagers in three-hour sessions on their own. These sessions were in Southampton, Eastcote, Newcastle upon Tyne and Bristol.

We didn't want the interviews to be biased because of our own personalities, so we asked three of our colleagues to help us, and in the end the interviewing team comprised three women and two men. Every session was tape recorded and transcribed so our analysis began with a pile of transcripts a foot and a half high!

People feel more at ease in surroundings not too different from those at home, but it would have been naïve to have expected teenagers to talk freely when Mum might have walked in at any moment. So interviewer and kids all met at the recruiter's house, shut the door firmly, and with plentiful supplies of food and canned drinks, and the floor littered with magazines, toiletries and chocolate bars, settled in for a four-hour session.

Each of the groups came back for another four-hour session a week later, and the feeling forged between the group members was so strong that no one failed to make it.

We started off with a rough checklist of the areas we wanted to cover, such as family, school, media, shopping, but this was only a base and the kids themselves chose what to talk about.

We established trust by talking ourselves, but we took care not to influence what the kids said any more than we could help. It is always possible to argue that while the kids we talked to were interesting, they might not be representative of teenagers in general. Obviously we couldn't interview every teenager in the UK, in order to put those we did see in context, but here again market research techniques came to our rescue. It is possible to select a sample who are statistically representative of the teenage population, and ask them to fill out questionnaires about their attitudes. This isn't as sensitive as talking to kids in person, but it can give you a lot of additional information.

For this purpose our network of recruiters dispensed 520

questionnaires from Torquay to Glasgow which the kids took away to their bedrooms and filled out in private. (The questionnaire included several cartoons with blank bubbles for the teenagers to fill in as they thought best. The samples throughout the book are some of the best ones that came in.) To give you an idea of the scale of the research – national opinion polls typically survey 1,000 people over an age range of 18–80 when they predict the election results. Our sample surveyed 520 people over an age range of six years. This means that any figures we quote are statistically representative of the teenage population and deviate no more than five per cent from the figure we would get if we interviewed every 11–16-year-old in the land.

In Britain, the working classes outnumber the middle classes by two to one, and our questionnaire sample followed the same ratio. It included children from one-parent families, only children, racial minorities and children with mothers who go out to work. The study was as complete as we could have made it.

Let's go back and meet the rest of the kids.

Picture Sarah, Beverly, Janice, Debbie and the two Judiths. They are eleven and twelve. They look like big children, fresh faced and pretty with neat glossy hair and little gold studs in their ears. Like the boys, they are wearing jeans, shirts and sweaters. At first they are shy and giggly, but they don't stay put for long. They are falling over themselves to tell stories about their mums, their teachers, and their brothers and sisters. They are going to grow up to be stable girls or champion gymnasts. In their exuberance, the only way to describe a disco is to get up and dance. They are shouting, giggling, eating, talking and dancing all at once. Very soon they are going to be teenagers; nothing could be more exciting: they will wear high heels and go to parties and date boys. Once on the subject of boys, they cannot be diverted: 'Please miss, can we do it all on boys?' I am astonished at their urgency. They are demanding to do things for themselves. What they know already is based on school and television. They go quiet when the conversation reaches a subject like divorce, or periods or rape; which are serious, but only half understood.

By the age of fourteen the serious side has overtaken them, life is a minefield of embarrassing situations. Think of Suzanne, Alison, Joanne, Sally, Liz and Heather in the North. They are too self-conscious to bring up a subject and too scared to answer a question. From the way they look, they could be eighteen, tall, slim, and blonde, wearing the universal jeans and sweater, but from the way they talk, they are crushed by problems. The group becomes a painful exploration of why they don't feel confident, why they can't wear what they want, why they can't talk to boys, why they can't talk to people. They are afraid they won't get their exams, afraid of looking like a 'slag', afraid that too much will be expected of them, afraid that their periods will start in the classroom, afraid of the future. They seek refuge in eating, ice skating, swimming, television and, above all, their friends at school. While they are working out how far to sew up the splits in their satin pencil skirt, they are cramming down chocolate marshmallows. It reminds me of bits of my own adolescence.

At sixteen, Michelle, Mary, Jane, Kim, Anya and Sue in London have taken a leaf out of the boys' book and covered the uncertainty with bravado. They have an image to keep up. They are wearing earrings and bright colours. They tint their hair, and Michelle has designed her own hairstyle which is short on one side of her head and long on the other. They have Saturday jobs and money to spend. They are experimenting with sex, drugs and drink, they have fought in the streets and they make me feel inadequate, when I think of myself as a teenager.

But they have buried their problems rather than resolving them, they are still anxious about how far to go with their boyfriends, worried what Mum will think, afraid of bullying, scared of dirty phone calls. But confidence is built on track record, and already they have drunk Martini and lemonade in the pub, survived a pop concert and put themselves on the Pill. If the world treats them as adults they can just about cope with it.

They see me as a source of information. I have reached my early twenties on the strength of my own decisions so my opinions are thought relevant. They want to know if I have sex, what marriage is like and what sort of job I have, and I can answer, knowing there is common ground between us.

As a woman, I relate intuitively to what the girls are saying; much of it I have felt myself. But the boys are a different story. I am understanding things for the first time : how they struggle for status; how they scrap for the fun of it; how crucial it is to be a *man*. It makes me think that if I never fully grasped the male point of view, then the chances are that men have never fully grasped the woman's point of view either.

At twelve, boys are much more immature than girls, but by sixteen they have pretty well caught up. Take David, Simon, Michael, Paul, Jason and Jimmy aged twelve; they are Mum's boys – they dress neatly and cheerfully, they never sweat and they never suffer from spots.

They idolize Kevin Keegan and sit glued to space adventures on the screen. They collect everything from beermats to belt buckles. They are macho without being sexy – it is a quiescent period; 'I'll wait to go out with girls, until I can do something about it.'

They range around on racing bikes, sprint to school in their trainers and watch hours of television. They parrot Mum's opinions on the state of the economy and saving for a rainy day. But this is the calm before the storm. Already they pass round Page Three and giggle, they lock themselves in the bathroom and make practice swipes at their upper lips with Dad's razor.

At thirteen and fourteen, the storm hits, they are out to prove they are men. Out on the street, into fashions, slapping on aftershave, looking for a fight. Life is one big dare, pubs, X-movies, nicking, scoring, smoking, big boots, spiky hair; a black leather jacket and an earring replace the cheerful sportswear Mum used to choose. Your mates count now.

And by sixteen most of the dares are done – they can pass for men. The excitement ebbs and Derek, Steven, Harry, Mark, Peter and Tom are talking about stability. They are used to drinking beer in the pub and staying out as late as they want to.

They know Mum and Dad can't do much about it, but they know they worry, so they make concessions from a position of strength. They assert their position among their mates too, as Skinhead, Heavy Metaller, sports enthusiast, joker, casual. On Saturdays they are on display down town in full cult regalia. They kid around, jostle one another, argue over bands and buy their own clothes. They are looking for their first serious girl-friend.

For the first time, they are coming face to face with responsibility; if they screw around, their bird will get pregnant; if they dress like a Skinhead, they will get beaten up; if they don't get their exams, they are headed for the dole.

They put a good front on it but they worry about the future. Being 'hard' does not guarantee you a job in a bank, and they see themselves more as the floor sweeper than the manager. They lack the skills to control their own future.

Every kid urgently wants to be older; some are physically credible and some are not; appearances don't necessarily tell you what is going on underneath. Teenagers don't absorb maturity like a sponge absorbs water, they flip at will from child to adult. The Punk, whose terrifying outfit frightens old ladies at bus stops, buys liquorice allsorts from his local sweet shop; the little girl who wants to be a vet is sniffing glue.

Underneath it all, they are learning how to be independent, with Mum providing the stability which lets them do it. They are avidly chasing experience, but right from the start girls are less confident than boys; boys are the doers and girls are the worriers.

Look at the differences in energy at eleven. Boys are waiting for manhood and girls are fervently anticipating their teens. When they actually reach their teens girls become self-conscious and depressed, whereas boys explode into the fray.

It is well into the teens before boys are beginning to calm down and girls are beginning to nerve up sufficiently to talk to one another at all. Fourteen is a deeply impressionable age – it is very likely that statements such as 'Girls are soppy' and 'You leave the conversation to boys' will become polarized in adulthood as 'Women are less able to take responsibility' and 'Men should take the lead'.

9

All the time, teenagers are trying to work out where they stand in relation to other people. They need to know what the extremes are, so that they can decide where, along the line, they fit in.

This is the first time they have been faced with *choosing* what they want to be. Their concepts are black and white; maturing is understanding the shades of grey. The next step is to find out how the concepts connect, and what that implies.

Imagine learning to use the London Underground. You emerge at Oxford Circus, with no idea how you got there; on to Marble Arch – same thing. Stations are like concepts, dotted all over the place, with no obvious connection.

Now if you look at the tube map, you can see that the Central Line connects Oxford Circus and Marble Arch. This is a start. The lines on the map provide enough connections for you to get where you want to go. Concepts work in the same way – once you have a framework, you can use it to explore new ideas. But the tube map is not the whole story – on its own, it would be a very thin picture of London. You really begin to understand London when you have walked from Oxford Circus to Marble Arch and looked at the shops along Oxford Street. You make connections of your own which aren't on the map at all – the only way to find out that Marble Arch connects up with Hyde Park Corner is to go down Park Lane and see for yourself.

All the experiences into which Karen and David and Stephen and Michelle fling themselves are gradually giving depth to concepts which start off as just words. Karen wants to be slim and has learned about nutrition at school but she lives on a diet of Monster Munch and Chewitts; Michelle at sixteen, is starting to ask Mum for brown bread and green salads.

David is horrified to find that the bank is lending out his precious savings because he thinks that each pound note is kept out of harm's way behind bars. 'They might *lose* it,' he says. But Stephen understands that the bank is paying him interest for the use of his money, and he is busy comparing interest rates across town. Understanding the concepts – nutrition and the financial system – means that Michelle can be slim and Stephen can be rich. It is the first step towards controlling your own life.

And there is a vast variety of concepts to master. Bombarded by school, the media, advertising, the pop scene, Mum, Dad and the lady next door, teenagers are forced to make decisions earlier than ever before. There is no set path, they are spoilt for choice, and they insist on sampling it all. Home becomes doubly important as a port in the storm.

But teenagers are living with a paradox. On the surface, they are being offered the world, but when it comes down to it, the world can only accommodate them in set patterns.

This book gives the kids the chance to express their feelings and voice their opinions. It is their words which say it best. As you go through the book you will hear Sarah and Simon speaking for the eleven- to twelve-year-olds, still children at heart; Ian and Beverly chiming in for the thirteen-year-olds; Tina, Joanne, Debbie, Andy and Kevin arguing through the confusion they feel at fourteen and fifteen; and finally Michelle and Harry, recognizably adult, tying up the issues at the age of sixteen.

What they say is in this book not only because they said it, but because it represents the feelings of many other teenagers too.

2 Family

Do you picture today's teenagers as leather-jacketed rebels shouting out their opinions on sex, drugs and violence? Do you shudder to think of them beating up sub-postmistresses and fainting over rock stars? Do you expect them to rear up in purple punk and denounce their parents' generation with contempt?

My mum says

Imagine for a moment what they would be like without their mums. Andy at fifteen would look pretty sad roaming the streets without a bed to go back to; he wouldn't be able to read the *New Musical Express* if Mum hadn't got him up for school every morning; he'd never make it to a date if Mum hadn't washed his Wranglers, and bought the family shampoo; he can eat his heart out for a Harley Davidson 1200 but he won't get it on £4 a week unless Mum teaches him how to save and how to negotiate a bank loan.

Michelle at sixteen flaunts her independence, but it's Mum's influence which stops her leaving the party pissed and pregnant. She claims to want the house to herself but when she picks up the phone and hears heavy breathing she panics without her mum. Without Mum, she faces the embarrassment of buying her own Lillets. Without Mum, she would be the proud owner of a pair of pink loafers and no clothes to go with them.

Simon at twelve would come in hungry after football to find nothing in the freezer, and instead of watching television he'd be trying to wash the mud out of his kit. He'd get very cold sitting on the road to Dorking with a puncture if Mum wasn't there to rescue him in the car. He would be very scared if the police picked him up for shoplifting and Mum wasn't at home to intercede.

Beverly at thirteen would have wasted her birthday money

on high heels which would have pulled apart of Mum hadn't pointed her towards a better quality pair. If Mum hadn't told her diving instructor she couldn't go swimming this week, because her periods had started, she'd have died of shame. Her friends would have laughed at her eyeliner in the disco if Mum hadn't been there to say, 'Don't put a lot of that muck on!'

Every other sentence begins, 'My mum says . . .'.

'She's an angel flying in heaven with me on her arms,' says Andy.

'She's my best friend,' says Michelle.

'I couldn't live without my mum,' says Beverly.

Life without Mum is unthinkable, it would be hollow, cold and dangerous. There would be no one to care whether you came in at night or not. Your mates are a laugh, but your mum will stay with you through thick and thin. Life with Mum must be wonderful, then.

'I can't see eye-to-eye with my mum on anything,' says Andy.

'She called me a tart the other day, so we haven't been talking,' says Michelle.

'It's always my mum who hits me and she's always shouting,' says Beverly. So life with Mum can be full of frustration too. The kids want to be out where the action is, messing about with the gang, going to parties, staying out late at the disco, playing the space invaders machine at the pub or singing cheeky songs at the Arsenal–Southampton match.

'We want to be older than we are,' says Beverly. 'We want to be able to enjoy ourselves instead of being stuck in the house.'

But Mum won't give them free rein until she's sure they can look after themselves. Mum hands out the privileges and lays down the law. Each teenager has to work out his own deal with Mum and then stretch it as far as it will go.

Sarah at twelve; 'In the summer I can stay out a bit later. In the winter I am only allowed to stay out until about 5 p.m. It's not fair:' If she can talk Mum into letting her go to the disco, then she can stay up till 9 p.m., provided her dad comes to fetch her.

Andy at fifteen: 'I stay out quite late now with my mates – about 10.15 in the holidays, as long as my mum knows where I am. I'm all right if she knows I'm round a friend's house. I've stayed till 11 p.m. sometimes. But not if I'm on the streets; she doesn't like that.'

Mum is worried more about her daughter than her son. She's twice as likely to say No to going out and twice as likely to check up on her when she does go out. Daughters have to be twice as devious.

Joanne: 'If you're going out somewhere, the last person you tell is your mother. But if I don't tell her and she finds out, she'll be even madder than ever. I just wait until I get her in a good mood.'

Look at the lengths Michelle, sixteen, has to go to: 'We were in this boy's house. I knew my mum would be a bit funny about it, but if I said I was staying at one of my friends', she wouldn't mind. Me and Sophie said first of all, we would stay at each other's houses, then we changed plan. I said I was staying at her house. Next thing my mum's ringing me up, saying, "Her parents know nothing about it." I said. "She never asks her parents." My mum said, "All right then." Then when I didn't turn up at her house, my mum says to her dad, "Make sure she stays there." When I didn't turn up, they said I was staying at Judy's, so he said, "I'd better tell her mum," but he couldn't get through, thank God.'

Harry at sixteen is past this kind of intrigue. Short of tying him down, there's not much his parents can do to keep him in and he knows it. 'If I tell them roughly what time I'll be in – I just get in then. It doesn't matter what time. Once I got in at 3.30 in the morning. They didn't do anything.' They push Mum as far as she will go but they don't resent her setting limits. On the contrary, it shows that she cares about them. 'Mum has a right to worry,' says Michelle. 'If your parents didn't worry they would not be fit parents. If I come in late my mum starts screaming; it's only because she's worried.'

Ever since they were children, Mum has been the big disciplinarian. She used to stop them running out into the main road, she taught them to brush their teeth and she bandaged their grazed knees. Now she stops them smoking, looking too sexy and hanging round the streets at midnight. Like Beverly's mum:

'She always says to me, "What would you do if a man stopped you in the street and he would think you was older than you are?" and then she says, "What are you going to do now?" and you'll just stare, so that's why I don't put a lot of make-up on.'

They don't take Mum's orders lying down though. Mum is so preoccupied with worrying about safety that she misses the niceties of teenage culture. She refuses to buy Harry a pair of baggy red trousers because she thinks they're outrageous, and buys him a pair of Marks & Spencer jeans instead. She doesn't realize that Harry is a Soul Boy and that no self-respecting Soul Boy could lift up his head without red pegs. Joanne wrangles endlessly with Mum about clothes: 'She doesn't want me in tight skirts. I said, "I'm not wearing a flared skirt." She says, "You're not wearing a tight one." We want the same things, but I want it a bit more the way I want it. She wants it more the way she wants it.' But going against Mum over something serious puts the fear of God into her. 'If I got pregnant, my mum would kill me. She says if I ever got pregnant, she'd put me in a home, but I don't think she would. She's just saying that.'

What it comes down to is that Mum has the final say in matters of survival and Joanne and she fight it out over the traditional teenage issues, friends, fashion and music. As Harry says: 'I have arguments with my mum – not serious ones though.'

Talking about Mum is not like talking about football or fashion, where teenagers can articulate their views simply. Since Mum is knitted into every aspect of their lives, she raises strong emotions. Comments about Mum can be contradictory, and sometimes incoherent. It is astonishing how much notice they all take of Mum, even the tearaways. Outwardly, Andy and his friends were the toughest group of all and this is what they had to say when I asked them what Mum was supposed to do:

Andy: 'Keep me warm. Keep us in order.'

Kevin: 'Look after you, until you're of an age to look after yourself.'

Andy: 'Your mum's got a right to know some things. They brought you into the world, then they got a right to ask questions. But if you don't want them to interfere, they shouldn't.'

Kevin: 'For help, if you were desperate, ask your mum for advice. You can always turn to your mum.'

An American psychologist put a two-year-old in a strange room full of toys and watched him through a one-way mirror. Left on his own, the toddler moved no more than three feet. With his mum sitting there, even though she didn't say anything, the child explored the whole room and played with the toys. Mum has been acting as launching pad for a long time.

Where's Dad?

By now, you may be asking – what has happened to Dad? This is a puzzling question. If Mum is the launching pad, what is Dad? The space station? Mission control? Government funding? 'I could get anything from my dad,' says Michelle, 'and he doesn't ask questions. My mum always wants to know what time I'm going to be in, where I'm going, addresses, etc.' In comparison with Mum, Dad is a shadowy figure. He doesn't get involved in the blood and guts of day-to-day discipline, so his role is more open. Dad can have a special close relationship uncomplicated by the nitty-gritty. Michelle's dad for example: 'I can talk to my dad. I can talk to him freely, more than my mum.'

Or Harry's: 'I get on best with my dad. He's interested in a lot of my hobbies – like football – and he goes to a lot of places with me. You have a laugh with him, like say you have a girl who keeps looking at you in school. You tell your dad and he has a joke about it.' Or he can be a benign stranger, like Sarah's: 'I think I'm closest to my mum really, because I see my mum more often than my dad. My dad's usually at work all the time, and when I get home, my mum's home, but my dad's not home. Sometimes he works at weekends.'

Or just not interested, like Andy's: 'Dads don't do much. At worst they hit you and that'll be it, but mums – shouting at me.'

17

Andy is upset and covers it with bravado. It is like a replay of James Dean in *Rebel Without a Cause*. First he won't talk about his dad, 'boring subject', then he runs him down: 'My dad gets drunk on Saturday nights', 'He's bald', 'Worn out now at fifty', 'Gives us his wages every week, then off he goes', and then gingerly: 'I wouldn't mind him teaching me to drive or something like that', 'He don't really ignore you. He knows you're there', 'He should take the lead and make all the decisions in the family. Earn the living', 'My dad doesn't drink unless it's whisky. You name the brand, he's had it.'

He ends up bragging about his dad. Dad is a hero. Andy aspires to hard drinking, driving a car and earning money as well. He too wants to be a man. He gets a kick out of borrowing Dad's shaving gear and he wouldn't be ashamed to be seen down the pub with him either.

Joanne can't copy Mum in the same way, because Mum is a law-giver, and teenage girls end up playing a more deferential role. Joanne learns to look pretty instead and waits until she has children herself before establishing discipline. She becomes a teenager before she becomes a woman, and takes her cues on how to dress and behave from magazines and television, rather than from Mum.

Mum takes a stand on all the tricky issues, smoking, drinking, drugs, clothes, make-up, coming-in times, sex, and Dad backs her up, when he's around. The issue where Dad has most say (and most difficulty) seems to be sex. Both Mum and Dad have problems accepting that their teenage children have sex anyway, but Dad really gets worked up about it.

Andy, fifteen: 'My dad would kill me if he knew I'd had it off with my bird last night.'

Joanne, fourteen: 'My mum doesn't mind me wearing pencil skirts but my dad does. I bought these jeans and he says, "No, you're not having those, they're too tight." '

And Dad has a field day when his son brings his girl-friend home: 'First time I went out with a girl, I came home and my dad kept taking the mickey. You're embarrassed to bring them in front of your dad because when she goes out, he goes, "Pah, you've got a right one there." '

For the kids it was even more embarrassing talking to Dad

about sex than it was to Mum. Simon was wriggling with embarrassment when the Anna Raeburn Show came on the radio while he was driving with Dad. Michelle sits in the kitchen talking to Mum about sex for hours, but she clams up when her father comes in. Beverly, thirteen, *hates* her father seeing her nude in the bath. I had the general feeling that whereas Mum had right-of-way on the tricky issues, Dad had visiting rights only.

But that doesn't stop family politics. Every kid knows which parent is the best bet when an ally is needed.

'I hate my dad and I think he hates me. I argue with my brothers and sisters and he always takes their side.'

'My dad usually sticks up for me, if there's something I want to do.'

'My mum says it's OK, then tells my dad.'

'My dad was going to hit me and my mum only just stopped it.'

'I saw the Blondie tape in W. H. Smith and asked my dad for it. He let me have it.'

Teenagers know how to manipulate their parents to get what they want.

Losing someone

Home is where they feel most comfortable. It's where they are loved, worried about and known, if not always understood. They brag about being part of the family. Beverly has the family temper, Sarah is just like her mum and Andy has his 'mother's nose'. They need the family round them, and girls especially are scared of being left alone. Michelle: 'I'd end up on the phone all day. I really can't stand being on my own. I'd rather sit under the stairs with my dog. You always think of scarier things ...'

They are terrified that somebody in the family will die and leave them.

Beverly: 'I came home from being out and my mum and my dad told me my uncle had died. My nan had died. I was close to my grandad who's dead now. They all died, a month after each other nearly. I'm afraid my mum will die ...'

Michelle: 'I'm not scared of death for myself. But I'm scared of death amongst my family. I just don't want anyone in my family to die.'

They are ready to believe in ghosts, reincarnation, the ouija board; anything so they don't have to accept that someone precious has gone for good.

Imagine, then, how they feel about divorce.

'Her mum's had a divorce,' says Joanne about her friend Debbie, 'and she's a bit funny. She's a bit soft, she seems as if she's a bit gone. They swear at her and she doesn't do anything and their house is an absolute mess.' The kids on the outside dread it and the kids on the inside wall themselves in against further shock. When she lets down the defences, Louise, thirteen, is in turmoil :

'I never thought my mum and dad would split up. I had this feeling and my mum kept me off from school one day and took me down to this house ... All that Sunday we had been out in the snow and we were playing and my dad kept throwing snow at us, and on the Sunday night they started arguing. They argued for hours and hours and I couldn't get to sleep. We used to live in this house called "Butterflies", for families in distress. Every night for two weeks, I just sat watching my mum. We had only three beds in this little room, we all had to share beds and I was so upset I just couldn't sleep. I started going down on the Saturdays to see my dad. I used to take it on myself and my mum hit me for blaming myself. And when she hit me I ran off, I didn't know where I was going. I just went anywhere just to get out.'

Listening to your parents fight is unbearable, you imagine they are arguing about you, you don't know what it will lead to. You can take any amount of violence and gore on the telly, because it is fake, but real violence at home is horrible. How can you see things in perspective at thirteen, when your parents fill the picture? 'Your mum and dad argue and you're frightened of them splitting up, and in the end, they never split up. My mum and dad nearly split up once because the dog we used to have used to do its business all over the house. We had to keep cleaning all the carpets. My dad must have got upset over something else and he left us for about two days. We really thought he'd gone.'

In the teenage culture, you never have to face issues this serious. Mum and Dad are meant to protect you, but if they fail then there's nowhere to run except inside yourself.

Louise: 'I'm frightened of both of them, I don't need a dad, I don't like him.'

Beverly: 'Watch what you're saying, Louise.'

You don't know who to trust any more. If you transfer all your allegiance to Mum, then sooner or later, a boy-friend will come along and dislodge you. If you open up to your new dad he might go off and leave you too.

Tina: 'There was this other man, but it was horrible. He was going out with another woman as well as living in our house, and he made this woman a £100 cheque in my mother's name. I was dead upset 'cause I liked him.'

The kids who watch their parents' marriage fail recoil from the thought of marrying in the future:

'I'm never going to get married.'

'My mum and dad have had another row again and that puts me off.'

'I don't think I want to be married, divorce is awful, you always regret it.'

But they are dead set on creating a happy home for their children:

'I'm not bothered if I'm rich or poor, it's just to be happy really. I want my kids to be happy.'

'It's best, even if you don't want children, to show that you do want them and be nice to them.'

The girls talk about divorce more than the boys do. Does this defuse some of the anger? What happens to the boy whose hero father walks out and leaves him? He covers the hurt with bravado. Does he then take to delinquency, according to popular theory?

The boys are far less inclined to talk about it but Mike, fifteen, talking from a middle-class background, thinks yes:

'The middle-class kids are the *fake* rebels. They're the ones who have got something to go back to if it doesn't work out. These other kids, if it doesn't work out for them, they've got nothing to go back to. Some of them have broken families, their parents are divorced.'

Me: 'Are they more or less likely to go in for violence?'
Mike: 'More likely than your average middle-class rebel.'

Young parents

Divorce forces kids to see their parents for the first time as real people, with their own desires and problems. Scared inside, their next step is to sugar-coat it all with reason:

'Mum likes her own way, Dad likes his own way. It wouldn't have worked out. Mum never went out before, only once or twice with her friends. Now she likes going to parties. She never let us wear make-up, but when she married again she didn't mind. She'd never let us have our ears pierced. She knows what to get us for Christmas now and all. My sister got gold earrings.'

But it is unsettling to watch your mum grow young again, law-givers can't start acting like teenagers.

The mums of our teenagers are in their mid-thirties and they want to look and feel younger than they are. Who wants to be dismissed as a middle-aged mum at thirty-five, and be left out of the fun? Thirty years ago Mum was expected to sit at home, do the cooking and cleaning and defer to her husband. If she does that now, people criticize her for being lazy, and anyway the family income goes down by half. Domestic law-givers turn into Prime Ministers these days.

But Mum's teenage daughter can't stand it. While Michelle is struggling to prove that she is a fully fledged teenager and different from Mum, her mum is wandering around dying her hair pink and wearing mini-skirts. So where does that leave her? Michelle is bitter about mums who poach on teenage territory:

'My mother, she's doing it the wrong way round. She's got really curly hair, she's just had her hair permed. She's trying to get all the pink bits into her hair. She's like thinking, "Oh the kids nowadays, they don't respect anybody else." All we're doing is getting on with our own thing. We're not disturbing anybody else. But you get mothers who want to join in and they just won't fit in, 'cause they've been brought up differently.'

Mum is a yardstick by which maturity is measured, but it is

no good having a yardstick which moves along with you because you can't gauge how far you've come. It is up to Mum to be consistent, so that Michelle can set up in conscious opposition. Not that she won't get criticized for it of course.

'My mum doesn't even french kiss. Honestly, she's that naïve. She just doesn't have any idea of anything.'

At this point, Mum can't win. All she can do is weather the storm and comfort herself with the reflection that underneath her sons and daughters know she has their best interests at heart. But if *Mum* feels in two minds about acting her age, her children are even more confused.

Half of each one of them wants to be cuddled, fed, anointed with baby lotion and saved from their own tantrums, and the other half wants to sleep with their girl-friend, ride a motorbike to London and drink with Clint Eastwood.

'I'd rather be out with my mates,' says Beverly, 'but I love to have a cuddle with my Mum now and again.'

Breaking away

They are bursting to grow up and do things for themselves.

'I like making things on my own. If I'm stuck I don't like people doing it for me,' insists Sarah, twelve. 'I don't mind them telling me but I don't want them doing it for me.'

She senses that her parents want her to stay young as long as she can. She doesn't want to hurt them, but she has scented freedom and nothing is going to hold her back now.

'I wish I was sixteen already, but like my mum says, "Don't grow up too quickly because you only get once to live." But I want to be sixteen *now*. I want to be seventeen really. We are little children, but when we are in our teens we will be growing up into adults, women. We will get more mature as we get older. A lot more manners.'

Joanne saves up for a 'boob tube' with her own money and hits the disco. Kevin gets his bootlaces nicked by the police outside the football ground. The place to experiment with independence is away from home, where people are more likely to treat you as older. You can't expect Mum suddenly to stop treating you like a child, because she knows you too well. Besides, if she did you'd have nowhere to run to when things went wrong. 'It's nice to think that people feel that you're older and don't treat you like kids any more,' says Joanne cautiously. 'It shows that they have that bit more confidence in you. But they overestimate you sometimes and think you can change overnight.'

Too much responsibility too soon is a worry, not a privilege. When Joanne tips over on her new high heels, or the gang finds out that Simon thinks *semen* is a sailor, they have enough trouble on their hands coping with the embarrassment, without having to come home and put on a front for Mum as well.

Of course, Mum doesn't do your image much good outside the house. You can't trust her to preserve your adult dignity in front of your friends.

'I used to get embarrassed when people saw my mum,' Harry remembers with a shudder, 'and these girls came up to me that I knew. I was so embarrassed. I was about twelve at the time.' Joanne has no choice but to go shopping with Mum, because she hasn't got the money to buy all her clothes herself, but it isn't easy: 'I say, "Mum, I'm not a kid." I'll go to town, and in the middle of this big shop, my mum will call, "Come on ducky." I say (through clenched teeth), "Shut up Mum."'

Bit by bit, Mum is relegated to the house, Michelle goes off to all-night parties and Andy spends his Saturdays parading up and down Carnaby Street. The more Mum is kept out of the way, the less she understands what her children are getting up to and the less she can control them. Worry makes her irritable and she clamps down on the obvious target – friends.

Stephen explains: 'I was allowed out later when I was younger, because at eleven I was just over the park, having a muck-around with my mates. My mum knew that I wouldn't get into any trouble or anything because I wasn't with a crowd that was known for that. But now I've started wearing fashionable clothes and going round with other boys in kind of gangs and everything. They reckon that it's all bad and everything – so I have to come in earlier now.'

Mum likes 'clean and tidy' friends and criticizes the scruffy ones whom she distrusts. But her children have chosen their friends themselves and such criticisms hurt.

Mum might be your best friend but you can't tell her everything. She simply won't be able to advise you on what to do if you are walking along the street in your Mod gear and a gang of Skinheads is closing in from the other direction. Sometimes you'll have problems just because you do things she expressly forbids you to do. You can go to her in the last resort if you get your girl pregnant, but you can't ask her advice on where to buy the cheapest johnnies.

Brothers and sisters

This is where older brothers and sisters can be invaluable. They are a halfway house. They understand the pressures of being a teenager and they have first-hand experience of dealing with Mum. Mark had a close relationship with his older sister: 'I like my sister. She told me all about sex. When I was about eleven, I suppose. My sister wants me to have a good time. She doesn't mind if I'm with a girl and doing it with a girl. She does it herself.'

Joanne depends on her brother Duncan; 'It's not that I dislike my mum. It's just that she doesn't understand what I feel like I can tell Duncan better, 'cause he understands more. He can give me a better answer if I need to know something.'

Having an older brother or sister is the single most maturing influence on a teenager. If Beverly sees her sister wearing high heels, spraying on Charlie fragrance and staying out until midnight, it won't be long before she's clamouring for the same. If she's lucky, she gets hand-me-down clothes and make-up, as well as advice. She is full of admiration:

'My sister wears nice tight jeans, nice fashions. There are more places to go to when you are older. Going to the pictures – X-films.'

If you're unlucky though, like Debbie, your sister can make life a misery. 'My sister Tracy picks on me for everything I do. She's spiteful, you know. About two days out of the week we get on. Normally we just don't speak to one another.'

The trouble is, that while older brothers and sisters are like magnets, younger brothers and sisters are a pain. They hang round you begging to listen in, trying out your spot cream, pleading to go where you go. To the fifteen-year-old, no age merits as much scorn as being thirteen; having your younger sister around only reminds you that it's not that long since you you were thirteen yourself. But there is an unwritten law that younger children can look to their older brothers and sisters for protection. This cuts short a lot of bullying, like when Sarah and her friend were playing in the shed :

'Some boys were throwing stones and bottles at us. My sister said to them, "If you don't stop I will get the police." She called the police and they came down and took the boys to their parents.'

However much they fight in the house – and all of them think they come off worst in arguments there – brothers and sisters support one another on the outside.

First steps
Gradually, then, teenagers build a network of support amongst people their own age. Then they take a deep breath and consciously go out and smoke their first cigarette, buy their first illegal drink, stay out until 3.30 a.m. and sleep the night at their boy-friend's house. They know Mum wouldn't like it and they hate deceiving her, but feeling guilty is the price you pay for doing what you want. Tina, fifteen :

'My mum thinks you start off very innocent and it works up. The more you're with them, the more you get up to. That is right. That's why you say things that are untrue, you want to make them feel all right. You don't want them to worry. My mum doesn't know the truth about me. She thinks I'm a good little girl, but really ... She thinks I drink lemonade. I couldn't talk to her 'cause I'd let something out.'

In the end, the strain proved too much for Michelle. She gave in and confessed everything to Mum. Mum came through too :

'She seemed really shocked at first but then she started saying she was expecting it to happen any time now. It was her idea that I went on the Pill. So now I can talk freely with her. I can tell her everything that's been going on and whatever's troubling me.'

By proving she can do as she likes on the outside, Michelle forces her mum to reason with her as well as laying down the law. This is the discussion they had on smoking:

'She said you can drink, and sleep with people, but don't smoke till you're eighteen. I've still got the power to stop you and I'll do so. So she gave me a month to give up. So I did try, for about two weeks, not smoking. But I found rather than needing a cigarette, it was just the enjoyment. I described it to her and she had one. She doesn't inhale. And I said, "I like to have one under stress", and she said, "Wouldn't you like not to be dependent on them?" You don't really think of it like that, whether you're dependent or not. If you want one you just have one. She kept saying, "It's a drug." I know all about it, but I don't somehow relate it to me. Maybe one day I'll want to give it up, I don't think I can at the moment because you've really got to want to. She said, "If you haven't given up within a month, I'll take you to the doctor and he'll give you some pills." So I told her that I had given up and now I feel guilty. But I don't see what it's got to do with her whether I smoke or not. She cares about me, but it's my individual choice.'

Painfully, teenagers work out their own territory inside the house as well as out. Mum offends Andy by telling him off about some johnnies she's found in his room. He shouts back at her, not because she doesn't have a right to talk to him about sex, but because she was sorting through his private belongings. Mum has to learn that however much she itches to tidy it, Andy's bedroom is sacrosanct. In return, Andy has to respect house rules, he must keep down the volume on his cassette recorder and come in at the time he says he will, without resenting it as a slight on his manhood. Joanne's dad will come and pick her up after the party, but in return she must take her share of the housework.

Life at home is slow compared with life outside but home is where the 'rebels' feel most at ease. Beverly expressed it best:

'I think families are more important than friends,' she said. 'I mean you've got to have a family haven't you, to be happy? But friends are important too, because if you didn't have any friends you'd be sitting indoors all the time!'

3 Ganging together

Dress rehearsal

What is being a teenager for? A hundred years ago, Joanne would have put her hair up, lengthened her skirts, and changed from child to woman on her fifteenth birthday. Today, she can take a breathing space and learn to be a teenager first. Teenage is a dress rehearsal for real life. The young make their entrance as children and their exit as men and women.

If Mark had been a Masai tribesman, the elders would have bestowed manhood on him at fifteen and sent him off to hunt with the men. If he'd misjudged a lioness on the prowl, he would not have lived to tell the tale. In Britain it is less risky; he has to go to school instead, and if he fails his exams he can take them again. At eleven, Simon had to be home by eight o'clock at night; at sixteen he is drinking with Dad in the pub. At twelve, Sarah wanted to be a stable-girl; at sixteen she leaves fantasy land and takes a Saturday job at Woolworths.

Being a teenager means living through mistakes and learning how to sharpen up. By the time you get through, you should be able to make choices – refuse a cigarette if you don't want one, or decide for yourself whether £5 is better spent on a record album or taking your bird to the pictures.

Teenagers are not expected to get up to anything serious, they are participating in manoeuvres, not war. But a soldier is no use on manoeuvres if he doesn't take it seriously, and teenagers aren't going to learn anything if they don't take it seriously either. They do. They worry about fashion, music, school and the gang – details are all. Michelle used to be a Mod, but now she's a Casual, so she can't wear her loafers any more. Philip has the full Rocker regalia, but they saw him leaving Virgin Records with a Specials album, so he's obviously a poser. Simon won't muck about in class and is rejected as a 'snob'.

The youth culture is built on fun – image, dancing, dating, fighting, music, sensation. The seriousness comes in learning the rules to play by. Teenagers have to be up to the minute – be able to tell at a glance what a new sticker means, recite the third verse of Blondie's new release, and know by instinct that they mustn't be seen in a pair of FU's. They must make no mistakes. The catch is they don't learn anything unless they do blunder. For Simon and Sarah at twelve, savouring their teens greedily from the sidelines, everything is unfamiliar. Things are changing so fast that even Michelle and Harry, at sixteen, can't help getting something wrong. The penalty is crushing, agonizing embarrassment. When Joanne rang up her boy-friend and found she had been chatting away to his brother for five minutes by mistake, she went all hot and couldn't think of anything to say. All she could do was put the phone down, and rush up to her bedroom. She was convinced she would never face her boy-friend again. Embarrassment threatens you at every turn. Andy couldn't face his mates when he swam in the school team and ended up in the wrong lane. Michelle was mortified to run into her boy-friend in town, when she was carrying a packet of mini-pads. Harry was shamed when he asked a girl to dance at the disco and found she was taller than he was.

As if you didn't have enough problems, adults are always putting you in embarrassing situations too. They insist you come and talk to visitors when you can't think of anything to say, they tease you about your girl-friend, they tell you you're too skinny, they look at you when you walk into a shop, they correct your speech in public.

Still, at least the weapons are on 'stun'. Adults are looking after teenagers. Look at the law, kids can't have a cheque card until they're eighteen, they can't drive a car until they're seventeen, they can't get married until they're sixteen and as minors they can't be held responsible for anything they sign. In some ways they are beyond damaging themselves permanently.

The way to avoid embarrassment is to surround yourself with people you know, so they all join gangs. The gang is the cornerstone of the youth culture. The gang moulds girls into teenagers and forges boys into men. Its home is the school and its parade ground is the street.

Let's go with Sarah (11), Simon (12), Joanne (14), Andy (14), Michelle (16) and Harry (16) and see what it's like to be part of it. The gang operates in two stages. The point of the first stage is to get away from Mum. Sarah has achieved success when she has her neat ginger hair pruned into a spiky Skin cut like everyone else's. The second stage is to show *you* are different from the crowd. Andy has achieved success when he walks away from the gang who are throwing crisp packets at the teacher, and says, 'They are too childish.'

The first stage

It all starts when Simon and Sarah first go up to their Comprehensive, at eleven. They are apprehensive. They've heard rumours.

Simon says: 'Most of your brothers and sisters say it's horrible in your first year and everybody picks on you.'

Sarah says: 'At first I felt very outcast – people are bigger than you – like when juniors go up, there are bad rumours going round, about people getting beat up and everything, but it isn't like that at all.'

They feel isolated, unprepared, excited, scared. They've been looking forward to moving up to the big school for a long time, but it means leaving most of their old friends behind. School seems huge. Simon feels small. Mindful of Mum he sets out to pay attention in class – well we know what happens to boys who don't work. ('This boy in our class, he kept messing about and didn't get very good marks, so he left just before Christmas'.) He is just copying a sentence about Egypt off the board when a pea hits the back of his neck. He is outraged. 'They just fire pea shooters at each other and it's a *lesson*.' Pretty soon, there is an established group at the back of the class who are always mucking about. 'They just mess about for the sake of it – just thinking that everyone will start laughing at their jokes.' What is he to do? He soon grasps the fact that if he goes on disapproving he is going to be dismissed as a creep. Manhood calls. He crumples his first crisp bag and throws it at the teacher's retreating back. This is fun!

Sarah is thinking of other things. With the exuberance of a would-be Olympic gymnast, she bounds off to make friends with whoever she can. Once she is over her first nerves, she regards her new class as fertile territory. She gets talking to Jane, who is next to her in the alphabet, Debbie who likes gym and Alison who used to be at her old school. All over the playground, little groups of girls huddle together talking. 'My Mum says you can ...' 'Did you see what Simon Rowe did in history ... ?' 'Will your mum let you go swimming tonight?' 'Did you see Blondie on *Top of the Pops*?' The group natters incessantly, it pounces on new recruits and sulks when Alison goes off with someone else.

Sarah: 'We've just had a new girl, and what annoys me is, you want to get to know her, then Alison goes off with her, then another girl goes off with her. After a bit, you get to go with her and afterwards she ... gets dead happy.'

People are swapping from group to group and jealousy runs high. Sarah chooses Sharon as her best friend: 'We're not supposed to be saying it, but we are.'

The friendship blossoms outside school. Sharon invites Sarah to spend the night at her house. Thrilled, Sarah accepts, she is introduced to Sharon's mum, they have pizza for tea, they sneak into Sharon's sister's room to try on her high heels, they are allowed to watch the horror film on telly until half-past ten. When they go to bed, they are so excited, they talk until the early hours. Boys, holidays, brothers, teachers and problems, such as when Mum and Dad have been arguing.

'Say you're stuck, your best friend, she helps you; when your parents are always arguing, or say they are getting divorced, you can talk to them. I can just let it off my chest if someone else knows, if someone else is concerned about, like.'

After school, Sarah sometimes goes horse riding and Sharon goes swimming. On good days Sharon's mum might take them ice skating. In the holidays Sarah and Sharon team up with the rest of the gang and go window shopping in town. They try on all the clothes in Jean Machine and dream about the day when they will be proper teenagers. Says Sarah: 'On my thirteenth birthday, I am going to change completely – I can't explain!'

Simon meanwhile is being beaten into shape. What he needs is a proving ground, and where better than school? School is full of rules asking to be broken, the teachers are sitting targets. If he can get one over on the adults, doesn't that prove he's a man? The air is full of dares: 'If you refuse a dare, they think, "What a baby!"' Losing face is unthinkable. Even though he's not sure he wants to, he finds himself hanging over the staircase spitting on the head of the Maths teacher. 'Sometimes you do things you don't want to, just to be with the group.' But standards are high; you don't win status in the eyes of the group for nothing. 'Like the other night, a bloke went up to the school, climbed up on the roof and stuck a "For Sale" sign on the chimney.' Pressure from the gang forces Simon to the limits and beyond; there is no place for self-doubt.

Simon and his mates are terrified of being caught sneaking off to the shop in Geography, and exultant when they make it back with a packet of fags. Emotion this intense makes for strong group loyalty. Each gang member depends on the others to back him up although it's more than his life's worth to admit it. Without the gang, he gets scared again. 'I suppose when they're on their own, they wouldn't do it. I wouldn't dream of bumping a fellow with a chain, but when I'm with my friends ... Being with your friends boosts you. It makes you want to do things like that.'

The second stage

By the time Simon is thirteen, his class has split into rival gangs. In full flight now, the rivals challenge one another to fight. The playground is full of scuffles. Fighting is fun, but they don't really want to get hurt, and there are unwritten laws against knives and razors. They taunt and scrap and bluster, but little real damage is done. Fighting over, they retreat to the back of the bike sheds to light up and brag about their exploits. The scent of aftershave hangs over them; someone produces a well-thumbed copy of *Men Only*; shrieks and giggles fill the air.

On Saturdays, the pack goes hunting. They rally on their racing bikes and hit the High Street. They check out 'Mick's', a shop well known for its fashionable gear. The lucky ones are already sporting leather combat jackets and heavy boots, the others are working out how to get hold of them. They drop into a department store to play on the lifts. They race up and down the main drag, seeing who's there and what they're wearing, they stop in at the record shop, thumb through the albums. Suddenly they've had enough, and they pedal off *en masse* to see the game or cycle to another town, fifteen miles away.

On most weekday evenings Simon does his homework and sits in front of the telly, but on a good night he plays football, or goes up to the leisure centre with his mates. On the way back they stop in at the chip shop for a can of shandy and a bag of chips. They muck about on the corner of the street, handing round the can because they never have enough money to buy a can each. They linger until they have to be home. Sometimes they go up to the youth club, but it might cost them 25p to get in, so they can't go all the time. Simon's mate David used to belong to the Scouts but he's got tired of that now – too organized and 'petty'. Youth clubs are more fun, especially if they leave you to do what you want. You can play darts and table tennis and listen to the music. There might be a disco on, but David is too embarrassed to dance. For the time being he will leave that to the girls.

And what's been happening to the girls while Simon has been chalking up victories against the system? It's hard to believe that Joanne, at fourteen, used to be as exuberant as Sarah. Her periods have started, she's a fully fledged teenager now and she carries the weight of the world on her shoulders. She is crushed by lack of confidence. At every step she expects to be shown up. Someone will ask her something she doesn't know; she's afraid her new outfit makes her look stupid; she daren't walk past the road works because the workmen will whistle. Like a 'tharn' rabbit in *Watership Down* she is frozen to the spot. Imagine her panic on coming to a discussion group with me, and being invited to express her own opinions. Joanne and the other girls were so pent-up, that it was two hours before they could talk on their own, without curling up with embarrassment. It took Sarah's crowd about ten minutes.

Instead of embracing everyone around, like Sarah does, Joanne clings to the people she knows. The gang won't show

her up. Life with the gang is more fun. There's safety in numbers. She and her friends spend hours talking about clothes;
they plan out together what they can afford to buy. News about
bargains travels round the school at the speed of light. They
go shopping together, but they worry that the assistant is looking at them; isn't their money as good as other people's? They
swap sob-stories about trying to get a 'boob-tube' out of Mum
and they romance about boys. But Joanne's friends get jealous
and give her a hard time when she actually starts spending
time with her boy-friend. The girls long to get out of the house,
but they don't unless they have a special party, or a disco or
date to go to. They ponder it weeks in advance, seeking each
other's advice.

'What shall I wear?'
'My clothes aren't in fashion any more.'
'How much make-up should I put on?'
'Can I afford the busfare?'
'How late will Mum let me stay?'
'What if I break out in zits?'
'What if I come on?'
And these are life's high spots!

At school, the class is diversifying into personality types,
and the time is fast approaching when Joanne herself has to
choose what sort of teenager she wants to be. What are the
options?

Popular, clever, goody-goody, confident, sporty, muck-about,
fashionable, bossy, show-off, 'always with the boys', 'big-
headed', cocky, quiet, noisy. What does she have to say about
them?

'A cocky girl answers back and everything. She threatens
you, so you sort of like to keep on the right side of her.'

'They get on better if you get one that's quiet and one's
noisy.'

'There's one group that's really into all the fashion and that.
They put nail varnish on, they wear fashionable clothes and
that for school.'

'If you try and be fashionable a lot of people don't like you
because you're trying to show off, being big-headed.'

'They're always with the boys, and when you walk past boys and that they always giggle.'

'They mess about at dinner time and get the dinner ladies worked up.'

'I don't like bossy people because if you say you want to do something, they say, "I'm not going to do that." They just want to do it their own way, and you get left out. It's not very nice.'

'You don't get on with people because you're all goody-goody and never speak out loud – you're afraid of saying what you want to.'

'Snobs are less confident than what we are – clever, not interested in fashion. They're not allowed out. A lot of them don't want to be like they are. But that's their fault. You try and help them.'

'They're very confident of themselves really. They will stand up to teachers more than they should – a dare, sort of thing. I think when you're with somebody who's right confident, your confidence grows.'

After weighing it all up she decides that it is best to be fashionable (but not so fashionable that you make people jealous at school), steer clear of snobs and goody-goodys, keep on the right side of bullies, and if you're not too confident, attach yourself to someone who is.

The boys too are grappling with the gang. Being 'hard' is what counts. At fifteen Andy has moved gangs a few times. He used to be leader of a group of 'weeds', but there's more status now being a 'middle man' under the toughest bloke in the school. Each group boasts a leader, a second in command, a 'funny man', a 'weed' and a load of 'middle men'. The leader is hard enough to beat up any antagonist if he has to, but he can't fight six at once. If he oversteps the mark, the gang will beat *him* up. The system is delicately balanced and built on aggression.

Andy and Kevin explain it to me in patient detail. Simon is a weed and Mark is a middle man.

Andy: 'There's tough characters and weak characters. There's a leader sort of thing and you sort of follow him, and then there's the bloke you can kick around, he's the middle man. He's not too tough and not too weak.'

Me: 'How does someone become tough?'

Andy: 'You get a reputation, if you know someone who is hard, then you get someone who is beating him up. You let them go and they automatically think you're hard. Some people come to your school – you know they've got an older brother. The older brother gives you a good reputation. Everyone worries for a few months, you know. You start getting beaten up and no one takes any notice of you then.'

Me: 'What qualities keep someone at the top?'

Kevin: 'If they're hard on someone else they've got strong characters as well. I mean, they're not sort of silly like – a bloke like Tucker Jenkins, if you watch *Grange Hill*.'

Me: 'Would this leader wear fashionable clothes?'

Andy: 'Not always – sometimes. You've got a lot of tough blokes who wear all these clothes which have gone out about a year ago, flares and things like that.'

Kevin: 'Some of them are laughed at, some of the tough ones are, but they'd probably punch your face in.'

Me: 'What do they do if they're laughed at?'

Kevin: 'There's really not a lot they can do, not if there's a group of you. Only they know the others in the group will get you if you laugh at them.'

Me: 'What's the role of the weak one?'

Andy: 'Trouble. He starts trouble and runs off and hides somewhere. They start an argument between two people, then go stand out at the side. If there's a fight, a hooligan jumps in, except for the right person who started the argument in the first place.'

Kevin: 'It sounds like one of my friends. He's the tough one and I'm the middle one and he was always calling me a skinny twerp. He was always making trouble and then, when it came down to it, *he got done in*, and he went home. That was only because he was relying on us.'

Andy: 'The weak one always tries to impress the others in certain ways like smoking. He thinks he's smart because he smokes.'

Me: 'What about the middle men?'

Andy: 'These are usually the brainy ones, who know more than the tough ones. They're usually smart, active, tough as well. The tough ones aren't really interested in being smart and active. The tough ones are a bit of a bird brain.'

Me: 'Who do you follow, then?'

Andy: 'Well, the toughest bloke in our group isn't really the leader, because he's thick, silly and stupid. Then there's the second toughest bloke and he's the sort of leader, but we don't always follow him. Sometimes we sort of take the mick out of him, but then he sort of beats us up.'

It is a highly sophisticated set-up. Kevin is an air cadet, and he and Andrew are both talking about joining the Armed Forces when they leave school. By the look of it they won't need any mental adjustment at all!

I ask them how they assert their individuality.

Kevin: 'You hang around with one group and you find that group isn't really good enough. So you duck that group until you find the right one. I mean you go into one group, get beaten up and then go into another group to see what that's like.'

Andy: 'Say you were a middle man and you're not really enjoying being a middle man, but you want to be a leader. Then you can change groups and be a leader in a different group. So if you change into a weaker sector, sort of thing, you've got all these weeds about. Then you can lead them sort of thing.'

Me: 'Are you serious?'

Kevin: 'Yes. It's true. If you don't like one group, you can go to another group. It will rank you down at bit, but you're a leader of them. Sometimes, being a weed of a tougher group (I mean being the smallest out of them, they're not older than me) gives me more enjoyment than being a leader of a weedy group.'

Although the boys would never admit it, much of the violence is bravado; ritual, not real.

Now that they're so highly organized, Andy and his mates are ready for action. They are out on the street at every opportunity, though Mum doesn't allow them as much freedom as they want. They've finished with 'stupid' and childish dares like setting off fire extinguishers and ringing doorbells. They know their own neighbourhoods forwards and backwards; they know how to avoid the local pouf; they know which off-licence will sell them beer; and they know the cinema with the best AA and X films. Off they go. Andrew brags about the time his mates got him in to see *Quadrophenia*, by squeezing him through the back window of the men's toilet – three storeys up. Kevin describes with relish how they took a dartboard up into the vicarage roof and some woman screamed at them and set the dog on them. 'Excitement is everything.'

Says Kevin: 'Barbed wire won't stop kids of our age. We want excitement. Walking around is boring. Playing football is good but it can't last for ever.' They fantasize about knives and guns, and if they meet a rival gang in the street, they are honour-bound to fight it out. They posture more than they harm each other because they are afraid of real violence. Andy makes sure nonetheless that he doesn't walk the streets without his mates to back him up. Andy must work his way through a standard list of dares in order to prove he's a man. Every time he achieves one, he favours the group with a lurid description of what it was like.

The dares are tied to a legal age restriction, the principle being that if the authorities let you get away with it, then they must reckon you are older than you actually are. Andy must notch up: being served an alcoholic drink in a pub under-age, getting into an X-film, asking a girl out, 'scoring' with her and smoking cigarettes. A less daring measure is to get himself a good part-time job. Andy gauges each attempt with the utmost care. It requires precise judgement based on how big he is, whether he's shaving yet, whether anyone small is with him from the gang and in some cases the cashier's reputation for leniency. If he gets chucked out of the pub or the cinema, he will never live it down. He would have to be very tough to bash his way back to the top.

Being different

By the time he is sixteen, Andy will have proved himself and be ready to move on. At sixteen, Michelle and Harry see the world in a more similar light than they have up to now. Harry has calmed down a bit and Michelle has been working on her confidence. They're both finding it irksome to conform to the group all the time. They want to be different.

Michelle: 'Most of them have done it because it's the in-thing, because that's what everybody else does. But I'm getting into myself, I want to be myself. I want to get into what I want, not what everybody else does.'

This is where teenage cults come vigorously into their own. Michelle and Harry are looking round for ways to be different, and here they are, ready-made. In 1980 you could be a Mod, Rocker, Punk, Skinhead, Soul Boy, Rude Boy, Two Tone or Hippie. All it took was liking the right music, following the bands, having enough money to buy the regalia and enough confidence to wear it once you'd got it. Boys take cults more seriously than girls do, just as they take the gang more seriously when they're younger; the leftover violence transfers to cult hostilities. Harry's friend Mike was a Mod. He earned the money for a pair of loafers, tonics, red and white socks and a target for the back of his parka, and went down to Brighton on the back of somebody's Lambretta, to fight the Rockers.

He said with wonder: 'My dad, when the Mods first came out in the sixties used to have a Lambretta. He used to take my mum down to Brighton!'

Michelle is more interested in cult fashion than she is in the underlying philosophy. She's pleased Mod is in because it has smart, flattering clothes and nice accessories. But that doesn't stop her claiming full cult identity. 'I am a Mod,' she says; not 'I wear Mod clothes.'

Teenagers absorb information about cults through the pores of their skin – they all know that Skinheads stand for anarchy, Punks are out to shock and Rockers are the heavies. Stop any teenager in the street and they can recite unerringly the uniform of any cult you care to mention. But only some of them have the confidence (and the money) to wear the full regalia.

Harry is more reserved than Mike – he aspires to being more fashionable than he actually is. He contents himself with a parka and a few badges; he doesn't want to risk looking 'stupid', nor does he want to draw too much attention to himself. But Mike loves it; he is down Carnaby Street every

Saturday afternoon 'posing' and whistling at the girls. Punk is too extreme for almost everybody. 'You'd have to be stupid to go out with green hair,' but 'They wouldn't hurt a fly. It's just the way they look, so evil.' Harry admits that at least they're original, and then complains that adults often make the mistake of thinking all teenagers are like that.

Michelle experiments. She and her friends try out images together. She isn't a loyal Mod, she wants to be 'different but not too different', she wants to be provocative, innocent, sophisticated, sexy and original all at once. 'You can't be different on your own, 'cause you end up looking like something anyway,' she laments.

School has faded for Harry and Michelle. They are both anxious to get their exams but now they are thinking about getting jobs rather than challenging the rule of the classroom. These days, Michelle is more likely to spend her evenings having a drink with her boy-friend at the 'Club Focus' than down at the disco with the gang. Dating takes up more time, music and the music cults are a Godsend – you immediately have something in common to talk about, if you meet a nice boy at a party.

Before leaving the subject of friends, I should say a last word about the poor 'snobs'. Throughout this whole period they are outsiders – deprived. They don't muck about, they don't join the gang, they don't smoke, they don't wear fashionable clothes, and they don't roam the streets. Listen to what Joanne has to say:

'At school, they don't wear anything fashionable. They talk different. They don't go out anywhere and stick to their work. I think it's the way they are brought up. I think they have a more sheltered life. They're not allowed to do things as much as we are.

'I know someone that, if her parents wanted to talk, she was sent out into the garden and treated as if she was always too young to know about anything. Her mum and dad would never let her go anywhere, even with me. And this girl's mother didn't like another girl that I used to go around with and she said if I ever took her round to her house, I couldn't be friends with her daughter. Well, no one is perfect, not even their daughter.'

Where do the 'snobs' learn all the things which other teen-agers learn from their friends?

4 School

In the first nervous sessions with the boys and girls, I started off talking to them about school because I thought it was the easiest way to break the ice. Once we began, though, I quickly realized that school was the key to understanding the adolescent.

A young teenage girl walks along a huge, white sandy beach on a dream-like tropical island. To us it is an idyllic picture and so it is to her mother, who feeling slightly self-satisfied asks her daughter what she is thinking about. Her daughter replies: 'I was wishing I was back at school again' – and she means it.

Why is school so important to the young, what does it mean to them, and why can holidays be boring?

Fun

School is exciting, it's alive, vital, full of young people eager to learn – not just their lessons but what life has in store for them. Almost two-thirds of the young people we talked to described themselves as 'very happy at school'. At school they have no personal responsibilities; that comes later, when they leave school. Now, they want to have fun. School can be fun because you are surrounded by kids of your own age. You speak the same language and although you may dress differently, follow different bands or live in a different part of town, there is this close affinity in being young and at school. It is a common bond that rarely occurs in adult life. Ian, a fresh-faced boy of thirteen living in the London suburbs, expressed some of these feelings:

'I say, "great, the holidays," and then you get halfway through them and you say, "I wish I was back at school again," you get bored. I like school when I'm in it.'

For Michelle and Carol, two vivacious, outgoing members

of their gang, it was this social life of school that they enjoy so much: 'If it wasn't for school you wouldn't know hardly anyone, would you?' 'It's fun being at a big school, you get to know more people, you walk around saying, "Hi, hi, hi" – and you always know everybody and you can mix with different people all the time.'

Apart from the lessons, there's always something going on at school, and Michelle talks about the frenetic activity she finds in a large London comprehensive:

'There's always something going on, it's fun, a laugh, a bit of excitement, something to do – otherwise it would just be your lessons.' She loves her school. I wonder how she will feel in a year or so when she leaves it and starts work.

A place to learn

They learn a lot at school, as Beverly, a young-looking second-year, slim, with long dark hair and dressed in the uniform of tight jeans and a sweatshirt, described so well; 'Most of your influences you get from school; you're here most of your life, you learn to swear, to smoke and learn what growing up is.' These teenagers are very conscious that they were innocent 'children' when they started their first year at secondary school but by the time they have reached the fifth year they are more confident and feel they have passed the main hurdles of adolescence. In the network of the gangs and groups that meet in the break times they learn about and teach each other the real facts of life, not just sex but also the experiences of drinking, smoking, drugs, dating, periods, shaving, contraception, shop lifting, fighting, cheating – all those things you don't learn in books or get told by Mum. Lessons about sex however are the most popular: 'I think all the kids like *Mayfair*. If you get a kid bringing *Mayfair* to school, you get about thirty kids all gathered round.' They counsel each other on family arguments, vendettas with the teacher, love affairs, how to cope with jealousy, bullies. 'We just sit around and talk about problems ... all sorts of problems. We sit around in a big group, there's boys and girls, and they ask for advice and we sit around and talk about it and try to help. It can be anything they're troubled about, even help with their homework, or it could be about world problems.'

Some learn early lessons in politics, how to become a leader and keep your authority and power in the eyes of the gang members. Others come to terms with being a middle man, and how to move round successfully or change groups to gain status. They build up tremendous loyalty in their gangs and support and protect each other against attack – both verbal and physical. Huddled in those groups in the corridors, around the radiators, behind the toilets, in the playground corner, at the bus stop, they are learning about human relationships.

School is a microcosm of adult society. One aspect of this which may be less obvious is school as the market place. Teenagers are interested in fashions and trends. They are always on the look-out for what is new, what is happening now, and they try to be the first with the latest in clothes, hair styles, records, dance, words – or anything else that is interesting. School, by the nature of so many young people being there together, becomes the arena for showing off the latest discoveries and acquisitions. 'If a crowd at school said have you heard that one, you have to say yes, so as not to feel embarrassed, and then I'd go home and listen to it.' 'If someone at school says that's brilliant then I'd go out and buy it – I usually go by what people at school say.' Even if it is not possible to show them because they are at home, they talk and brag to their friends. They talk about the best place to shop, what makes a good bargain, how to earn extra money. What seems to be common these days is using school as a place to buy and sell. The most fashionable trendsetters will sell their clothes and accessories to another kid who has only just discovered that style – the trendsetter gets the money to move to the next fashion and the crowd follower gets a bargain. Money is tight for these kids and they have to hustle to get it. Records are frequently bought, sold, swapped or taped, and boys with the collecting syndrome will swap and buy from fellow collectors.

All this goes on during the break times and it conjures up a picture of a bustling bazaar with the children out on show, exchanging information and ideas, buying and selling, swapping collections, hustling over money and prices, generally showing a great deal of ingenuity.

Lessons

That is the social side of school, where the young are learning to grow up, but they view the academic side in a different light. They start secondary school at eleven, full of enthusiasm and eager to learn. They are embarking on new subjects such as languages, science, mathematics, literature, the arts. They are excited as they realize that knowledge of these new subjects is another of the rites of passage into the adult world. This thrill is apparent no matter what their background is.

'I love discovering new things.'

'At school you find out about things you wouldn't have expected, like geography, learning new things about different countries.'

'School makes life more interesting, if it wasn't for school you wouldn't be able to do French, German or Biology.'

But something seems to happen and for most of the children this initial thrill gradually disappears. By the time they have reached the fourth and fifth years, disillusionment has set in. Compare the previous comments with these.

'You get a bit tired of school.'

'They treat you like a child and you get bored.'

'It's boring, you have a set timetable, the same lessons each week.'

Why is this energy and lust for life missing when it comes to their lessons?

The blame must lie with teachers and the educational authorities. This may seem an unfair condemnation particularly as the press is always telling us about classroom violence, truancy and the low pay for teachers. But truancy and violence seem to be just examples of the kids' frustration and symptoms of the inadequate teaching they receive. Children may not be able to judge the quality of their lessons but they do know whether or not they are acquiring knowledge and basic skills. Their views about teaching are surprisingly mature and consistent – regardless of their age, sex, the home they come from, or the type of school they attend.

46

They know what is wrong, but it is only when they are close to leaving school that they realize the implications and grow bitter. The following are some of the comments the kids made about their own teachers.

'He just puts it up on the board and we copy it down every week.'

'I just get bored, he's always going off the subject ... telling us about when he was in the Navy, who cares what he did in the Navy!'

'Some teachers couldn't care less whether you do well or not. Our geography teacher gives us work to do and then goes off, and when you can't understand what you've copied down he says, "That's too bad!" '

'Our science teacher is useless, he has to keep looking it up in books all the time or asking the head of the department.'

'The strict teachers know how to put a stop to us, but with the others everyone mucks around and then they try and teach through all the noise. Our English teacher is hopeless, she can't stop us.'

'I just chose the subjects I liked and where they had good teachers ...'

'I just get bored at school, I can't sit still for long or I fall asleep. You don't get anything interesting to do, it just doesn't appeal to me.'

The last quote was from Debbie, a fifteen-year-old Mod from Leeds – she couldn't wait to leave school. What does come through from the kids is this sense of boredom and dullness; yet they themselves are so full of energy which they want to have channelled. By comparison the teachers were static, they don't seem to respond to the liveliness of their pupils, they don't seem to care that the kids need exams in order to get a job when they leave. Harry was a slightly bitter sixteen-year-old from Leeds who was disillusioned with school: 'Some teachers couldn't care less whether you do well or not, and if you put your hand up for help because you're stuck they just belt you round the head.'

Simon lived in a nice suburb of Manchester, he looked typical of the boy who had not long left primary school. He was full of enthusiasm for his new school and he was enjoying the challenge and thrill of new subjects – they are widening his horizons – and although he looked a child to me he felt he was beginning to grow up. But it was with disappointment that he described the response from one of his teachers: 'In our current affairs lesson she just gets us copying words out of a dictionary and finding out what they mean. Then next week we have a test on them. We've been doing that for five weeks now and it's a bit boring.' Compare this teacher with the presenters of the news and current affairs programmes on television. They make their programmes interesting and stimulating and the young like them and even rate them amongst their favourite programmes alongside *Dallas* and *Top of the Pops*. They like *Horizon*, *Tomorrow's World*, *Life on Earth*, *World About Us*, but see a wide gulf between these and their science lessons at school.

Children of all ages consume a tremendous amount of television, it's on all the time and is a source of entertainment as well as education in the broadest sense. 'You learn all about how people really live in all those other countries and you see it on the news too.' They also pick up what is happening from the other media: newspapers, radio, magazines and cinema. They know what is happening in the world, indeed they cannot avoid it. Modern technology is no mystery to them and they accept it as fact. The young have been born into the age of the computer and they are sophisticated enough to see that school frequently stands back from progress:

'Why don't they teach us about computers, explain them to us? They even make cars with them now.'

Kevin is right, but conversely many teachers fail to get over to their pupils the relevance of traditional subjects such as history, languages, literature, geography. The kids are continually complaining: 'What's the point of learning history? It's all in the past.' 'Latin is a waste of time, you're not going to go back in time and speak to a Roman unless you become a monk.' 'I have trouble learning French, but what's the point? They all speak English.'

What's the point? Does anyone ever tell them? These subjects would have a lot more interest if they did.

Debbie, a bright fourteen-year-old living in Bristol, mentions a good example of the benefits of positive teaching: 'Since I've been learning economics I understand what they're saying on the news, it all makes more sense to me, it's about everyday life, it's helped me a lot.'

Her friend feels the same about geography: 'We get out a lot and go and see things, that's when you learn about things. You can see how the country has changed.'

But sometimes the messages between school and television get interpreted in unlikely ways, and this conversation between two thirteen-year-old boys shows some of the naïvity of the young:

'I can't see the point of religious knowledge.'

'No, it's necessary – it improves your knowledge, for instance when you hear the news reporter say, "Oh there were bombs again in Israel today," If you hadn't done RE then you wouldn't know about Israel – you see it improves your general knowledge.'

Sexual stereotyping was evident but it was in the practical subjects that teachers had both made an effort to try and change this as well as attempting to explain the reasons why. Cookery was often taught to boys and woodwork to girls, and this seemed acceptable – 'Especially if you don't get married for a while; it will save you going down to the chip shop every night' – but some boys needed a justification, an excuse to prove their masculinity was not in question: 'Skinheads do cookery ... it gets them out of lessons and you could always tell people you throw eggs at each other.'

Comprehensive schools seem to provide a fairly wide curriculum for these pupils but one problem is timetabling. Often subjects clash, so something has to be dropped, which is disappointing and likely to limit future career options. There seems to be little consultation between staff, parents and child about choice of subjects. When a choice is made the boys and girls are often swayed by the teachers themselves – choosing those who are good at teaching their subjects. Again, this indicates the maturity of the kids but is worrying if they are making unwise choices: 'I chose the subjects I liked and that the teachers are good at.'

Teachers

Depressing though the general standard of teaching seems to be, there are of course good teachers – and they are recognized by the children. Boys and girls of all ages agree that a good teacher is strict, consistent, fair, teaches the subjects well and interestingly, is willing to help and advise, marks homework on time and, ideally, has a sense of humour. Such teachers are also the most popular in school and they gain due respect for their honesty.

If kids were as degenerate as the press suggests one would think they'd go for the softie teachers who let them get away with everything – but they don't. They like the teachers who lay down the rules or conditions and then abide by them. As Joanne says, with her basic teenage logic: 'That's their job ... A good teacher understands the children and doesn't lose his temper, he doesn't set hard work and expect you to get on with it without asking questions. He listens to what people say and makes sure you do your work properly – that's their job.'

For children, even at sixteen, see the world in simplistic terms; everything is black or white – grey comes later, and that's the next stage to cope with. They see discipline in terms of right or wrong, and while they have a keenly developed sense of justice, they have to accommodate their lust for fun and 'messing about' at the same time. They need rules but they will always try to break them – that's what rules are there for. Underneath, though, they are worried about their school work and exams, so are grateful for the strict teacher who makes them work and also relieves them of the pressure of having to attempt to rebel. This is most marked in group leaders, who are expected to be defiant and witty when up against authority. Michelle, although pretty, charming and likeable, can still be a real terror in the classroom. She attends a notorious London comprehensive and is a ring leader, yet her comments about a good teacher show the conflict about rules: 'A teacher must be strict or the class will run riot. I respect them when they have a go at you when you're doing something wrong. You will always argue back but you know they're right – they're doing their job properly.' Michelle is ambitious and wants to be a career woman, working in computers, but without the rules to hold her back she would run riot along with the rest of the class and would not learn.

Self-discipline is absent. The concept of freedom is admirable for adults, but there needs to be a framework to base it on. The adolescents are too young to accept such mature ideals. What becomes very clear is that adolescents can't cope with the responsibility of freedom and it is unfair to expect them to. For example Andy who is fifteen and at school in an area of London full of educational disasters, sees the discipline problem like this: 'If you want to learn, you learn, if you're not interested you drop out. Teachers, they say they're not going to kill themselves, they'll do their job if we do ours – that's OK as I see it.' The teacher feels harassed and attempts to be honest but it is unlikely that a fifteen-year-old will see the repercussions of 'dropping out'. If no one cares at home either, he will never get any qualifications. And he may not realize now how vital they are to getting a job. When he's twenty-three he may begin to appreciate the folly of his school days but by then it may be too late.

So discipline and control give teenagers a sense of security, a framework within which to learn. Eleven-year-old Simon and sixteen-year-old Michelle are years apart and in different parts of the country but they both show gratitude at the intervention of the teacher:

'There's always a class idiot. Ours is called Michael. They mess about all the time which is annoying because you're trying to get on with your work ... You need to have a class idiot, though. Some teachers just stand there yapping all day long and if someone makes you laugh and starts shooting pea shooters across the room it takes your mind off it and you join in.'

'A teacher must be strict or you run riot. They need to keep the class under control – most of our teachers can't. I like our form teacher, she's strict but nice and teaches us well. If she wasn't strict we'd have wrecked the class in a week.'

'You know whether or not you can mess around in a lesson. If you know you'll get told off then you do it in the other teachers' lessons. The strict teacher knows how to put a stop to it but in the others' lessons everyone mucks around and then they try and teach over the noise.'

The following lament about homework also illustrates the effect of discipline: 'If I get lots of homework I do the work for the teacher that is really strict but leave the homework for the teacher who's a bit soft and I just say "sorry" and they let you off.'

That comment suggests a degree of cunning among the young, and they can also be quite cruel if given the opportunity. Sarah is a sweet little eleven-year-old but she and her class can quickly turn into monsters: 'Young teachers can't control us. Ours, everyone plays her up and we get her all worked up and then she goes outside and cries!'

They can quickly assess new teachers and find their weaknesses: 'If a teacher is very unsure of himself you pick out the weak spot. I think children are more wicked like that ... you watch if they stutter, or the way they hold the chalk ... it can be just anything.'

Alongside the tacit need for discipline is the insistent plea for fairness. They want to be treated fairly, they want consistent discipline and consistent punishment when they break the rules. These 'rules' can be the school rules or the implicit rules of the classroom. They hold the greatest respect for rules that they consider fair – but will argue endlessly about the unfairness of illogical school rules or such phenomena as sixth-form privileges.

Many of the formal school rules they consider senseless, conjured up solely to causes chaos or to feed the power complexes of teachers and prefects. They are treated as thinking, sensible young people during lessons, but sometimes at break times treated like morons. Ian thinks it gives rise to aggression: 'School's OK but they've been going over the rules again and everyone's been going mad. There's been a couple of fights, I think it's because people get angry about the rules, they're small silly rules that don't seem to apply to anyone ... things like taking your coat off inside the school regardless of what the weather is like ...' Paul could not see the point of causing so much fuss about whether or not you wear your jacket in the classroom, and as he pointed out, if you leave a leather jacket in the cloakroom someone will 'nick it'.

Inconsistency within the teaching staff is a great cause of complaint. Debbie feels it unfair that one teacher will turn a blind eye towards smoking behind the tennis courts whereas another will give them a hard time: 'Some teachers don't mind, they know you're going down there for a fag but don't say anything, but my English teacher she got me suspended for it and I'll never forgive her for that.' Michelle complains bitterly about the unfairness of being picked on and singled out by a teacher for blame, but being more sophisticated than some teenagers she describes it as 'a personality clash'. Again, the most popular teachers are those who are scrupulously fair and treat everyone the same.

The children have problems coming to terms with hypocrisy. They recognize it but cannot really understand it. For instance, twelve-year-old Simon rationalizes his first thoughts about gambling and shows some of the underlying confusion about what is right and wrong; what is breaking the rules and what is not. He can't really cope with degrees of 'wrongness': 'It's silly banning gambling, because we have bets with the teachers about who will win the Rugby International. They worry about us playing "Penny up the wall" but not about us wasting it on the machines in the amusement arcade on the way home from school ... but I suppose if kids lose all their money and their parents find out they will complain and the school gets the blame. So they must ban it really – I suppose.'

Teenagers feel passionately about everything that matters to them, including their school teachers. Hatred and vendettas against teachers showed during conversations.

'Sometimes they're like an enemy to you and you don't go into the class to learn, but you go in to hate him.' This comment from Harry sounds bitter but it is really a sign of frustration, a lack of communication between them, and this is the only way Harry knows to express how he feels. Unfairness is usually the root cause.

The good teachers seem to have acquired the skill of communication between child and adult, usually because they are prepared to listen. Children are looking around them all the time and therefore have a lot to say but they don't get much chance at home as no one takes them seriously. In all my discussions with the boys and girls once they had got over their initial shyness and embarrassment they talked and they enjoyed it. I was an adult who encouraged them to express their ideas and listened to them. I was not there to criticize them and we built up an emotional bond. They all said how unusual it was to talk in this way to an adult; adults rarely asked them for a point of view. They made the same complaint about many teachers: 'Teachers like telling you things but they don't like it if you have something to say.' Contrast that comment with an assessment of a good teacher: 'It's someone you can have a laugh with but do some work too ... you feel more on a par with them, on the same level, and if they're like that you want to learn, you know they're there to help you.'

A good teacher understands the children and doesn't lose his temper. He listens to what people say and makes sure you do your work properly.'

It is interesting that when the teacher makes the effort then the children respond by saying they want to learn. There is no undertone of conflict when a good teacher is described, despite their strictness.

The ability to teach is vital for a teacher. The kids knew what good teaching was – it was making them understand a subject, creating interest and imparting knowledge. There were many examples of bad teaching, as when the children just copied down facts from the board. But for many of the children difficulties arose when they came up against their own limitations. Debbie realized how lucky she was: 'It's good being clever because you don't have to sit there thinking, "I can't do that, what am I going to do?" and all that – there are a lot of people like that, though.'

Others are not so fortunate ... 'It's all more difficult than I had thought.' 'As you get older they push you harder and expect more of you, but the trouble is when you can't do it.'

It is difficult to ascertain just how much the school is to blame for the thrill and anticipation at eleven turning to boredom and disillusionment at sixteen. After all we must accept that some children are not very bright, but the least we should do is let them realize their full potential. The good teachers do seem to try: 'Our maths teacher is really good, and she explains things to you and helps you – she will always listen if you don't understand and you can go to her early in the morning before assembly to get help.' This teacher is giving her pupils the benefit of her time and she seems concerned that they have the opportunity to grasp her subject. These young people I talked to have definite points of view about their teachers and the way they are taught. But unlike any other 'consumers' no one ever asks them what they think of the services they receive. In most schools there is no formal procedure for school children to complain about their teachers, unless a criminal offence is involved, so criticism tends to be left to grumbles amongst friends in corridors and in the playground. The comments they made to me, though, all sound reasonable and mature. It seems fair to criticize a teacher who 'just puts it up on the board and we copy it down – every week' or 'when you put your hand up for help when you're stuck and he clips you round the head'.

In most jobs the staff are continually assessed and reviewed, but how does this happen in teaching?

Harry was always vocal about school, he was one of the leaders who spoke his mind. He was bright but had not done too well in his exams and wanted to leave school as soon as he could. I don't know what his teachers thought of him, and why he was not so good at his academic subjects, but being the sort of character he was he did not sit back and accept the system. He wanted action, but unfortunately the drastic action he chose meant he was the one who would suffer: 'You get stuck with teachers, you can't get rid of them so all you can do is to be really bad in a lesson and get kicked out – it's as simple as that!'

Michelle, the ring leader with a highly developed sense of justice and rights, had attempted to complain to the head about some of her teachers and the way they treated her but the head had misinterpreted her motives: 'I tried to explain which teachers I got on well with and which I didn't and why, and he started calling me a slag and a slut, although he was putting it politely. He's got no right to do that, I really wanted to kill him. I was trying to be good and not be naughty in class – he had no right to say all those things about me.'

All these quotes and comments seem to point towards a general lack of communication between teachers and pupils, the school, parents, education authorities, the media. What seems to stand out clearly is that we underestimate the kids in this; they have a better idea than we think about the way they are taught.

Beverly's throwaway line sums up with humour the clarity with which they view adults: 'We should be paid for putting up with half the teachers.'

Comprehensive schools

Most of the young people we talked to attended comprehensive schools, but a few went to the smaller grammar or church schools. Comprehensives are popular with kids because their size provides a variety of friends, situations, subjects, teachers, classrooms and opportunities. The social side of school is more developed in a comprehensive because there are more people, which means there is always something to do, events going on outside school, parties, scandal, gossip, fights, etc.

'If it wasn't for school you wouldn't know hardly anyone.'

'It's fun getting to know more people.'

Gossip and scandal are just as popular in the classroom as in any advertising agency but comprehensives tend to have more fuel for talk. When asked what makes school exciting, the girls replied: 'Boys,' 'If something happens to one of the teachers ...' 'If someone gets pregnant. Did you know four girls have had babies in our school and none of them are with their blokes any more ... terrible ... and it's bad that it gets round so easily.'

Teachers are also the subject of gossip. It's bad luck for the good-looking games teacher when he's spotted with the new English teacher on Saturday afternoon; and if a teacher's silly enough to confide in a pupil it's all round the school by the end of the day.

Fights seem to happen all the time, particularly in the schools with a reputation, but when you talk to these boys and girls the fights seem to be little more than another form of entertainment; play acting for the benefit of the rest of the school as the audience. I was aghast to hear the nice girl with long red hair, who was worried about her freckles and whether or not she looked too fat in her jeans, describe to me some of the fights she had been involved in – but she had enjoyed them and was unscathed. What also fascinated me was the way Debbie described the build-up to the fight.

In a very large three-storey comprehensive school built in the 1960s, a maze of staircases, corridors, classrooms, everyone is working away, and suddenly the word gets out ... 'You can almost hear the whispering, you sort of hear it going down the line, then you hear people running from the top floor and the word gets round quick and they gather round and start shouting "Fight".'

Here is another example from the same school of the speed of communication and how the trouble and excitement starts: 'You know when we had that really hot summer, well me and the Skinheads, you know, Big John and that lot, well we decided to go on strike. We thought sod school, we didn't want nothing to do with it. There were about twenty of us sitting outside on the green, and at the first break we decided on a strike at lunchtime and so at lunchtime we sat down and then by the end of lunch there was about 900 kids sitting on the grass – the word had gone round just like that. I got into big trouble for that.' No word of the reason for the strike, but that's immaterial, it's the fun, in this case challenging authority, that's important.

Paul, a Mod from the other side of London, agreed with the idea of creating a spectacle: 'They like faking fights, a whole crowd of them pretend to have a fight when everyone's looking ... There's always rumours going round about what's happening – they say at that other school the boys have guns in their pockets.'

In the vast majority of cases it is harmless, just part of being young and having lots of energy to burn up: 'Steaming into each other, wars with the different factions at school, most kids enjoy it, it's all fun.' 'It's fun, a laugh, a bit of excitement.'

In comparison, the smaller grammar or church schools are boring. They are generally much quieter, and their smaller size means there is more control from the staff. The following comment made by Michelle was unheard of in Carol's high school three miles away: 'We go out at lunchtime, we're not really allowed to but they'd rather have us out than in, they almost encourage us to go to the café.'

The boys and girls from these smaller schools also seem quieter. Calling them dull may be unfair, but they do not seem to have this same ability to question, challenge, criticize or just make comments. They are more aware of their 'place', and afraid to flout conventions; less confident too. They don't seem to have any relationship with their teachers – whether for good or bad reasons. Due to the lack of challenge they are not learning about personality and how to cope with situations and conflict. They lack a certain vitality and brightness and appear to be waiting for the future rather than expecting it all now. What will happen when they all leave school?

One of the best things about most comprehensives is that they are mixed. All those at mixed schools really appreciate being able to mix with the opposite sex – Beverly, Andy and Sarah agree and yet show a great deal of sense in their reasoning: 'It's stupid to separate schools. I was watching a programme on public schools and they keep them separate so half the boys end up gay ... it's like you shouldn't go near a girl, you should get on with your education – that's rubbish, you should mix with girls, and pay more attention to your teacher.'

'I wouldn't like to go to the high school, they're boy mad and that's all they talk about, but in our school you learn to live with them and it gives you more confidence with boys.'

'In discussions in class if it's just girls it's the same thing but when you've got the lads there it's more interesting. Some are totally against women, but it's more interesting to get two sides.'

'It's good to have boys in our class. We just get along with each other, we argue and have pretend fights.'

'You're just used to them. It's normal. We all mess about together.'

Of course the romantic element exists, but they seem to appreciate the opportunity to really get to know the opposite sex. To learn to understand them, to see their strengths, weaknesses and qualities. They seem to get a sense of proportion about sex. Young shy girls like Mary learn to stand up for themselves: 'They call you fatty if you're fat ... they called me an old rat bag the other day but I didn't care. I call them something back now. I called Peter goofy yesterday and he didn't like it!'

The size of comprehensives has its advantages but also its disadvantages. At first, moving from a primary school, the first-years find the size terrifying. Not only are there thousands of pupils who know their way around the school but everyone is bigger than them.

'All the classrooms seemed enormous and I was going round in circles. It was very strange at first being in with all the big ones and it is a shock when everyone starts to pick on you.' It doesn't take long, however, to get into the swing of a big school: 'It was a bit of a shock at first because everyone picks on you, but it's good when you make some friends.'

'At primary school you're a prefect and boss people around, but now they boss you around.'

They like having a different teacher for each subject, it seems more professional and serious, but running around the school can be frustrating, as Simon describes: 'The trouble is you have to keep running round, it's not our fault the first lesson is music and then its RE which is the other side of the school and back again for French – it's like that all through the day. If only they'd make the timetable different we could get more done in each lesson.'

The size and facilities, however, provide the opportunity for some comprehensives to lay on extra-curricula activities outside school hours or during the lunch hour. These schools appreciate the social education side of school and there are often keep-fit classes, art and craft lessons, discos, film clubs, etc. which help the kids to get to know one another and to take extra classes purely according to their own interests.

Thus schools, especially the larger comprehensives, are providing the kids with their own society, and they enjoy it. This is why *Grange Hill* is such a popular TV programme – it mirrors their own lifestyle, it is personal and individual to the young, and adults are excluded. The young understand school, they know its rules and way of life and they feel secure there. Adult society is still comparatively unknown to them and underneath they are worried by it. Very few of the boys and girls we talked to said they wanted to leave school. They wanted to earn money and have a job, but the thought of leaving their own youthful society proved a dilemma.

Leaving school

Leaving school is something they had to face up to sooner or later. How do schools react to their needs and prepare them for life 'outside'? Even when they start secondary school at eleven the children are conscious that eventually they will be leaving school. They all admit it is the main reason for going to school.' 'If you want to work when you're older you have to go to school.' 'You've got to learn to get a good job, if you want to get a good job you have to learn.' 'If you're not serious about school, you can't do well when you grow up.' But it is in the future for most adolescents, so they are not that concerned, they're just paying lip-service to it. Time horizons for the young are much closer than for an adult; to a thirteen-year-old a year is an eternity. This means that the kids only consider what will happen to them when it is imminent and when they are in the fourth and fifth years of school.

Exams are seen as the key to future success: 'You've got to have your exams because if you don't take them you won't get the right chances of success. There'll be other people with better exams and they'll get the jobs and you're left out and that's not so good.'

Many of the teenagers quieten down in class when they begin to appreciate the importance of exams and the necessity to learn. It seems much easier though for the children from middle-class homes. Their parents, jobs, the homes they lived in, the holidays and the car are all signs of the rewards of taking education seriously. Their parents encourage them to get their exams, maybe stay on at school and consider further education. The children themselves appreciate that the longer you study, the greater the sacrifice, and the greater the rewards or the better the job.

60

For those from working-class homes there appears to be less encouragement or obvious motivation for achievement. Their fathers understand the trades or the factory production line but such jobs tend not to need exam results and the pay is much better in the short term. Therefore these kids are more reliant on their school for help and advice.

When it comes near the vast majority of these kids are genuinely worried about leaving school and getting a job. They don't really know what they want to do. All schools provide a career teacher but these vary. The schools only seem to be equipped to deal with the clever kids – they can just advise them to stay on and try for further education of some sort.

The problem lies with those who want to leave school and get a job. Judging by the comments of these teenagers, their teachers have little idea of what to advise and also little concern. Harry lives in Leeds and is getting near to leaving school; he still doesn't know what to do and has received little help from the careers teacher : 'They're not bad, but they don't have much to say if you're stuck for ideas, they don't really try and help ... they are only interested in those they think will do well in a job and they don't bother with the others ... You just copy it all out of a book, that's not much good.'

Teenagers such as Harry are in a dilemma because they want to get a job, but really have very little idea of all the possibilities – how could they? They may look like tough young lads and spend their time hanging around street corners, but in terms of the world they are innocent and naïve. They know nothing of adult life except what they see in the environment of home and school. It is at this point in their lives that they become aware that television doesn't really show 'real' life and people : 'I'd like to see people work, see what it's like because you can't just go into a building site and find out for yourself. You don't know what half the jobs are all about.'

Joanne feels daunted at the thought of going out into the adult world. She is shy but able to cope well within school and among all her friends, but she is decidedly anxious at the thought of a job : 'Working in an office, I wouldn't go to a meeting, I'd be too nervous, I couldn't face people. At school it's just you, yourself and now and then the teacher. You don't get to talk about things with people from the outside. I'd like to but I wouldn't know what to do.'

Yet girls seem to be more complacent about getting a job than boys; it isn't such a major worry for them, but then most of them are thinking they will get married and not need to work. Youth employment, however, does loom large in most of the kids' minds, and this is especially true for the boys in the North: 'It's a bit worrying, this chap the other day was going on about three million unemployed school leavers in $2\frac{1}{2}$ years' time and then there wouldn't be much chance of a job.' 'I don't know, it seems jobs aren't going to be too easy now.'

One way out is to try to get some exams – in their simplistic view of the world it is the easiest solution. This is why so many of them leave the decision of exactly when to leave school until they receive their exam results. If they pass their exams and a job is offered they leave, otherwise they stay on to take them again.

Even the decision to try to go to university is allied with job prospects; the idea of studying for the sake of it is not for them: 'I'm not that keen on school, but if I can't find a job before I leave then I'll have to stay on.' 'If I get my O levels I ought to get a better job.' 'If I get good results I'll get a good job.' 'University gives you a wide choice of jobs.' 'If I can I'll try and get to university because if you do you get more chance of getting a good job.'

While school is a vital element of the young society, performing both educational and social roles, it seems to break down in preparing the young for their future role in the adult world. I gained the impression of a big gap or barrier between school and society. The teenagers retain a sense of isolation, unsure about their next moves. Harry and Joanne expressed almost a panic at the idea of going out into the world of work. If they could they would cling to their exams – a life-support system, but what if they had none? It's at this stage that they begin to realize how ill prepared they are for the great unknown, and for some a sense of bitterness creeps in at the way they were treated at school. Why didn't they work harder? Why didn't the teachers make them listen? Why didn't school tell them how important it all is? Why did they choose the wrong subjects? Why didn't school show them what it was all about? – all questions that show a sudden realization that they are leaving school ill prepared. But why do schools appear to ignore that there is life outside school?

If schools were more integrated into society there wouldn't be this difficult leap from school to work, and they would be more effective at providing the children with the skills they need to exist in our modern society – with its new technology alongside the growing unemployment. The onus falls back on to the teachers, who are ultimately responsible for the education of the children they teach. The young of today receive a lot of criticism for being lazy and uncontrollable, but the vast majority of the boys and girls that we talked to and interviewed, underneath their boisterous exterior, showed a high degree of maturity and seriousness about the need for education. They entered school really wanting to learn, excited at the prospect of learning new subjects and discovering new facts and ideas. They knew they needed discipline, they were unable to discipline themselves so they had the highest respect for teachers who controlled them and were strict and thus gave them the opportunity to learn.

Although they are 'consumers' of school, unlike any other consumer in our society, they have no public outlet for their views about education, and even if they did they would probably lack the confidence to speak out. This means we must be more sensitive to the young and listen seriously to what they have to say about school.

'They like telling you things but they don't like it when you have something to say.'

'Parents can't help you, they don't know the way they teach today.'

'Mums always go back to their days when they were at school and they think school is like that today. They don't know.'

5 Sex

I am well-settled into the discussion with Andy and his friends (all fourteen and fifteen) when Kevin suddenly calls out: 'Have you got tapes of the girls? What did they say? I'd be scared to talk to them, I don't know why.' Everyone goes quiet and I realize he is asking a significant question. I have to think quickly. 'Well, they talk a lot about boys and you talk a lot about sex,' I offer cautiously, 'they're very embarrassed, talking about sex.' 'We're not embarrassed, are we?'

Without warning the discussion U-turns on to me.

'You could do a striptease.'

'You should have told us you were going to strip at the end.'

'Everybody would be excited.'

'We see you only as a sex object, not as an interviewer!'

Laughter.

'I am falling madly in love with you.'

Me: 'Aren't I a bit old?'

'No.'

'He'll take anything.'

'I fancy my teachers!'

I am delighted on the sly that they see me as a sex object! They begin to question me minutely on whether I wear make-up, whether I've had a baby, whether I count as a girl or a woman, whether I like my job talking to boys ... I can feel their interest, and I am amused at how delicately they tiptoe round, to spare my feelings, even though they want all the details. After some to-ing and fro-ing they decide that even though 'only slags wear make-up', the amount of make-up I've got on is exactly the right compromise. In spite of all their bravado, they know next to nothing about girls, but they want to desperately. I'm probably their best chance in a long while to find out. After all they can't really talk to Mum, they can't get near enough to a real girl and their mates aren't too sympathetic. Says Andy: 'I'd rather talk to you than some bloke, 'cause you can't say anything to him, 'cause he might start laughing at you. If you start to talk about girls or something, he might not understand, like you would if you're a woman.' I feel like big sister, *femme fatale* and Mum all rolled into one.

But what a contrast with the girls. When I ask Joanne and her friends about sex I am greeted with embarrassed silence:

Me: 'What about sex?'

Silence.

Me (trying to drum up a reply): 'Do you approve of having sex early?'

'No.' Silence.

Me: 'How does it make you feel?'

'I suppose I feel a bit embarrassed.'

'I don't happen to be bothered with it.'

'I suppose the prospect embarrasses me.'

'I don't think about it.'

All agree self-consciously.

Embarrassment stops them asking me questions about sex and boys, or dating, even though they talk about it endlessly amongst themselves. Their discomfort reminds me of the agonies I went through when I was fourteen. I am conscious that my confidence, and their lack of it, sets up a barrier between us. Whatever must it be like on their first date? It's a wonder they don't die of embarrassment before they get there.

Let's follow Joanne to a party and see what it's like.

The party is at her friend Liz's house and Liz's mum has let her convert the garage into a disco for the night. Joanne has been planning for weeks what she's going to wear. She spends half her time in school uniform and the other half in jeans, so parties and discos are the only chance she gets to look fashionable. Looking fashionable also means looking sexy, but she'd rather not think about that. She puts on her precious satin pencil skirt, which she pleaded for at Christmas, and last summer's T-shirt, then hesitates over the matching earrings.

Finally she brings out her latest prize, a pair of high-heeled Mod 'pickers' which she coaxed Mum into buying this afternoon. Now for the make-up; she doesn't want to look cheap, but she doesn't want to look too young either. Carefully she coats her eyelashes in mascara and smoothes on some glittery blue eyeshadow. Hmmm, not sure about this. A bit of blusher on her cheeks, then some lipstick called 'Gone Rum'. One look in the mirror tells her this is too much, so she rubs the lipstick off again. She doesn't want boys to get the wrong idea. She brushes her hair (it looks nice now it's blow-dried) and pirouettes self-consciously in front of Mum, just to check that she doesn't look stupid.

She's very excited. She's arranged to stay over at Liz's house, so she doesn't have to be back by midnight.

She picks up 'the gang' and they catch the bus over to Liz's. They all giggle as they go in, and take an appraising look at everybody's outfits, as they pick out a dark corner for themselves. Joanne is disgusted to see Liz's twelve-year-old sister capering round the dance floor in high heels which are much too old for her, and suddenly she begins to wonder if her own skirt looks too sexy. Embarrassed, she shrinks into her chair. Debbie pulls her out again to go and get a drink. She's not sure whether she should have a Martini and soda or stick to orange juice, girls look so awful when they're drunk and she doesn't know what effect the alcohol will have. In the end she settles for shandy and retreats back to her corner to see who's there. Paul and Andrew from her class at school are showing off, drinking beer. Andrew's all right though he doesn't look like much, but Paul is a real poser, dressed up as a Soul Boy when everybody knows he likes Mod music. They are laughing and messing about and Joanne dreads them staring at her or saying something nasty about her skirt. She's grateful 'the gang' is there to talk to, at least they're all dressed the same.

As she looks round, through the flashing lights and music she sees some boys she doesn't know – they must be friends of Debbie's brothers. They look like the sort who would put girls down. What will she say if one comes over to talk to her? It isn't easy talking to boys, they don't seem to have a lot in common. She's never had a steady boy-friend, although she has been out on dates. She was so nervous the first time she nearly didn't go. She knew he would expect her to kiss him and she wasn't sure how to. He put his arm round her and she was 'sick and tired' of it but then she let him kiss her ... she was worried though in case it led to something else.

The new boys look as though they would be a laugh, they have lots of confidence. She can hear them talking about ice skating, but she knows that she just wouldn't be as good as they are. If one does come over and talk to her, the best thing is to be natural, and try to find out what sort of things he likes; leave the talking to him. As long as she looks nice – is she fashionable enough? She wishes she had a new shirt to go with the skirt; is the slit in her skirt too high? Does she look like a slag? What if he asks her to dance and she tips over in her new shoes? She would be so embarrassed. If she dances with him, should she kiss him? Will he ask her out if she does? Boys aren't serious about dating, everybody knows they joke about it, she's heard about girls who have got pregnant and the boy has just dropped them. She fancies the one with the blond hair and drainpipe jeans, but he probably doesn't fancy her. That always happens; he's probably saying, 'Ugh, that old thing.' One of the gang offers her a cigarette. Joanne lights up gratefully, at least it will calm her nerves and make her look older ...

While Joanne is fretting herself into a state of nervous tension, let's take a look at what's going on with the boys. Chris (with the blond hair) and Mike are fifteen and they have come along to the party because the gang decided the night before it would be better than trying to get into to see *Alien*. They are hoping to find free booze (maybe there'll even be whisky if Debbie's parents are out) and some good music. (Debbie's brother is into Heavy Metal.) If there are some nice girls there, so much the better, but they can't enthuse too much or the gang will think they're going soft.

They stand around sizing up the talent, knowing it will do their status a lot of good if they can score with somebody. Chris got quite close to scoring once before with some slag on a campsite in Wales. She let him feel her tits, but unfortunately the fortnight's holiday was over before he could get any further. The gang had been transfixed as he bragged about the moves he had made – tits like Ursula Andress. So what if he had exaggerated a bit?

He watches Joanne picking her way over to the drinks table. She's got nice tits, nice face too, imagine what's underneath that dress! Mike'll be impressed if he walks over and gets her to dance with him. When it comes to it though, he feels shy – what if she turns him down with Mike looking? You can't rush things with a nice girl. He might risk asking her out if she lets him know she likes him. Then they can go to the pictures and take it from there. Of course if he does score eventually, he'll have to watch it, some girls want to get involved once they've gone to bed with you. His brother had a girl-friend who expected to see him every night and he just got bored. He wonders if Joanne's got a good personality. He used to be a bit self-conscious about dancing ... Mike dares him to go on over, he cracks a joke, picks up his glass and studiedly saunters off to try his luck.

The big difference between Chris's view of the situation and Joanne's is that Chris is the initiator. 'It's better as a girl, you don't have to ask him out, he comes and asks you.' They both feel shy, but Chris is so used to being dared by his mates that he puts his fears aside and makes the first move.

Joanne is crushed by self-doubt, far from getting up and doing anything, she sits and frets about her appearance instead. The reason for this is curiously twisted. At thirteen Joanne got her first period and from this moment on she is a woman in the eyes of the world. She has nothing to prove; her figure develops and pretty soon she can look as mature and sexy as she wants to, just by adjusting her clothes and her make-up. 'One girl who I know, she's about thirteen, put make-up on and high-heeled shoes and she got in to see an X-film.' And what's the result? She is scared stiff of being too sexy, because she doesn't feel able to cope with it. It's frightening to be a child one month and a woman the next, because you haven't yet learned how a woman ought to act. So Joanne swings backwards and forwards, thrilled that she looks grown up one minute, and afraid that she looks like a tart the next; putting on the lipstick and rubbing it off again. 'Between thirteen and sixteen, you get called a tart, but if you're twenty-five that's all right, you're grown up by then. Because adults do more than what children do, they have to go further to be called a tart.

Whereas a girl just has to kiss a few boys and she's a tart. To be just right is really hard.' Physically Joanne is equipped to be a woman, but socially she doesn't want the responsibility. So she opts for being a teenager instead.

Now for Chris it's just the opposite. There is no recognized event which abruptly changes him from boy into man. Is it 'making spunk'? Growing a 'tache'? Hearing his voice break? Nobody is quite sure. Physical changes are unpredictable. Meanwhile, his instincts are urging him to be independent and girls are beginning to look very attractive. If he doesn't *look* the part, the only way to be accepted as a man is to go out and prove it. And he proves himself through action. By the time his beard grows, he has already been roaring drunk, won a fiver gambling and bought a packet of coloured 'johnnies'. The biggest worry he has about sex is whether or not the girl will reject him. He might lose face. Unlike Joanne, he has no qualms about accepting responsibility, he's out to notch up as much sexual experience as he can get: 'Girls worry about getting pregnant, so you have to use a johnny most of the time, makes me sore, but . . .' Scoring with a girl is irrefutable proof that he's made it into manhood.

Both Joanne and Chris are talking about sex, long before they have any idea what the reality is like. Wherever they turn – newspapers, TV, magazines, pop songs – everybody's talking about sex and everybody assumes that everybody else is doing it. Imagine the pressure on Joanne: 'If you go out with a boy, after a few weeks he expects you to do what he wants like a dog. If you say "get lost", they think you're square. You won't let a boy do anything.' And how can Chris ever admit that his girl-friend wouldn't let him?

. Teenagers are catapulted from stamp collecting into sex before they have time to work out what it means to be a man or a woman themselves. What's more, they *expect* to make sexual decisions early, like it or not. 'If people start talking at school that they've never been to bed with anyone, then they'll look for someone to go to bed with for a fling at a party. I started sleeping with girls when I was thirteen,' says Harry (sixteen). 'Love is just sex,' says Beverly disconsolately at thirteen.

It might as well be Action Man going to bed with Cindy Doll. All they have to go on is a set of stereotypes about one another. School, family, television all offer conflicting views of what girls and boys are like, and trying to work out their *own* sexual identity first makes it even more complicated. The questions are: Am I a child or am I grown up? Am I really a man/Am I really a woman? Am I going to go to bed? What's the opposite sex like? – in that order.

Being feminine

Let's see what boys and girls think they're meant to be like and take a close look at some of the contradictions. First the girls. Sarah (twelve) sees endless possibilities for herself when she becomes a teenager:

'I might have periods.'
'I might be wearing a bra.'
'I might be all posh.'
'I might be in the fashion.'
'I might be a Punk with a pin in my nose.'

She sees women as vulnerable creatures with 'more delicate places than men, they might turn around and bash them'. Women lead a lurid life, loosely based on Mum's. 'They produce babies and the man sits and holds their hand while they're having it.' Then they plunge into a hard life, looking after the family 'before going off to have affairs with other men'. Sarah marvels at these goings on, but is not surprised. She accepts them as a child, they are part of the fairy tale. All she can do is wait until she's old enough for it to happen to her. 'We're not as attractive to men as women are, we're not mature.'

But Beverly (thirteen) and Joanne (fourteen) have already entered the fray. They are more concerned with themselves. Being a teenage girl means quietening down, 'giving up sports' and having 'more manners'. It means you get left out of the action, teachers stop choosing girls for competitive sports, and tough bike rides and leather gear are left to the boys. It means you have to 'look nice, because if you looked untidy, people'd think you didn't care for yourself'. It means saving up to be in the fashion because if you're not 'you're conscious that everybody's talking about it'. If everybody's looking at you, then 'your clothes must reflect your personality'. 'I want people to think I'm a lot of fun, nice to be with. If you wear sad looking clothes, they think that's what you're like.' Joanne wants to combine fashion with good taste. Above all she wants to be 'nice', 'nice slim figure', 'nice eyes', 'nice hair', 'pretty', 'nice to be with', 'balanced', 'nice personality'. Thinking about her image makes her uncomfortable: 'You're trying to act somebody else.' When she talks to boys she must strive 'to be herself', and 'treat them just like you'd treat anybody else'. Not so, Beverly, who's busy modelling herself on heroines of the silver screen:

'I don't want to be myself, you want to act as if you were a film star, say like Jaclyn Smith. I used to like Farrah Fawcett Majors. I always used to pretend to be like her. But now they call me Miss Piggy!'

But whatever image she adopts, she mustn't 'cake on her make-up' or look cheap. It's fatal to get a reputation as a slag: 'Rumours is another bad thing. Someone I know got drunk, went with this boy, didn't do anything, watched telly. The boy was trying to get off with her, but she wouldn't, so he went round telling everyone she was a slag.'

Joanne wants people to think she has a good personality as well: 'But personality isn't everything, people say looks aren't anything, but you know they are kidding you.' To hear her talk you'd think 'having a good personality' was the same sort of thing as having 'nice hair'.

Anyone who picks up a copy of *Jackie* or *Annabel* will recognize instantly this unchallenging constellation of desirable feminine qualities.

But Joanne, Beverly and Michelle have all been members of the gang at school and they know girls aren't all sweetness and light. They've suffered from girls being 'jealous' and 'bitchy' especially when a boy is involved. 'If you're catty and you say things to hurt people, calling people names and picking fights then people will be bound to talk about you.' They're scared that in reality they might develop into girls who 'nag' and 'get ratty'. Although they have high ambitions to go on to further education, they feel already that they are meant to look up to men. If Joanne challenges her boy-friend, she will be 'shown up'; her role in life is to find his good points and build them up. Let him take the lead and get on with the talking.

Happily, confidence stirs at the age of sixteen, and Michelle is talking about going into computers, even suggesting that she will earn the money if her future husband can't find a job. She hopes he won't be domineering. Already girls are in two minds about the way they're meant to be.

And how do boys see the girls?

Simon and his friends, at twelve, are uneasy about girls, threatened even. 'If they're better at football, it's a bit embarrassing. They're always trying to prove they're better than us. They do nothing really, just laugh their heads off and muck about.' But if he's honest he has to admit 'My little sister was better than me. She used to kick goals past me into the net – so I used to go off in a sulk.' If the worst comes to the worst you can always bring down the weight of convention on them: 'You just do your best to ignore them, but if you've got an important game, go off and tell the people in charge not to let them score. We're better than them.'

Tomboys are a fact of life. Grudgingly, Simon has to admire them: 'A tomboy I know did some daring high jumps to escape a man who was chasing us. *She* had to persuade *me* to take the necessary leaps!'

But this state of affairs doesn't last long. Tomboys change into girls and enter a mysterious private land, fringed with 'tits', 'periods', and 'having babies'. To Andy, it's as inaccessible as the dark side of the moon:

'I'd hate to be a woman, too many problems. Periods and all that. Having babies and all the torture they go through. I couldn't bear the pain. Periods must be painful as well. They disgust me really.'

As a physical body, a girl is a thing of wonder, almost any girl is good looking, but especially if she has a good figure. The transition from the pages of *Men Only* to a real girl is more of a thrill than getting drunk, seeing the home team win, being chased by the law, and sneaking into porno films, all put together. For convenience, they classify only two types of girls, 'either they're slags or they're nice'. Nice girls require careful planning. Andy explains:

'First of all you start kissing her on your first date, then after about two hours you try something else, sort of thing. If she doesn't let you then, you just keep kissing for the next four dates like that. Then you try it again. Then she might let you. I don't mean all the way, but she might let you touch her tits. Something like that. Then she might let you after a while. But you really shouldn't try it too quick because then they think that they're a bit free. That's a bit slaggish. They want to gain some respect off you.' Slags merit contempt.

So far they see girls as an uneasy cross between Wonder Woman and St Trinian's; so they round out the picture by adding in the qualities of the only other woman they know about: Mum! Mum is faithful, loving and caring, soft and gentle – well in theory at any rate. Girls should be 'soft', 'gentle', 'subtle', and 'faithful'. 'Wonder Woman's got a nice figure and a nice face.' 'She's totally devoted to her husband too.' 'I wouldn't like to have a wife having it on the side with the milkman.' They regard girls who break the rules with misgiving:

'In America you've got women pilots? 'It's not right for a girl to fight, is it?' 'They're like savages, pulling each other's hair and scratching, they bite. My sister had to have injections in her hand!'

Sadly they reflect how things are changing: 'Girls ought to sit down and say nothing, then you get the Prime Minister – just the opposite.'

So girls switch abruptly from being 'doers' to being 'supporters', and then edge back towards being doers. No wonder they feel ambivalent. They respect Debbie Harry as a sexy doer but they daren't follow her example. Every sex-related question from now on will reflect the same contradiction. As Michelle says, 'We would like to see ourselves as women, but we have to look at it in a different way now, with equality.'

Being masculine

Boys have a much easier time of it. Everybody expects the same thing from them. Simon, Andy and Harry don't spend a lot of time introspecting; they are usually in the thick of it. They want to be 'cool' and 'hard' and 'smart', able to 'handle situations' and able to hold their own if it comes to a fight. They don't sit around, thinking about doing things, they go out and do them. Their hero is Clint Eastwood, their ideal is Macho. They want to stand six feet tall, grow a virile moustache, and watch women fall at their feet. They sport the badges of toughness – big boots, leather gear and a knife. They want to be leaders, fighters, winners. They respect daring and a good sense of humour. By sixteen they'll be drinking whisky with Dad in the pub. They are wary about getting too involved with girls. They might look soft. Underneath, they are more unsure of themselves, but it's more than their life's worth to let on. They are used to putting on a brave front: sometimes aggressive; sometimes humorous; sometimes plain cheeky. But if you depend so much on appearances, it is a terrible blow if someone calls your bluff, especially in front of a girl, as Andy describes: 'All the blokes were there and we were here. We were fighting and then we stopped. Then the girls from their side went crazy. They were going, "What you stopping for?" and they were going wild and started to fight us, because the boys couldn't take any more. Too beat up.'

The boys are ashamed of their inadequacies. 'You worry about everything but you don't publicize it.' Five feet tall, fine features, downy cheeks – nothing could be more ignominious than having a girl your own age turn you down because she's bigger than you are. Who knows what women like anyway? 'They say big woman like, prefer little men, like Ronnie Corbett. I think they go for Cult men, like Elvis Presley, Charles Atlas, people like the Beatles.'

At twelve, Simon feels so inadequate that he shrugs off the whole thing: 'I'll wait to go out with girls until I can do something about it.'

In such a macho world, the one character who is certainly not going to make it, is a pouf. Poufs are universal pariahs, girls distrust them and boys publicly revile them. 'He kept looking at me, smiling. I picked up a stone and hit him in the eye, if God meant you to be a woman, you'd be a woman.' Even if Andy had been interested, it would be more than his life was worth to say so. Manhood demands an unyielding front and poking fun at poufs is obligatory. Constant bravado doesn't leave a lot of room for learning how to be tender. Boys apply the same social tactics – arrogance, humour and bravado – to girls as they do to one another. But the boys don't talk about it so the girls fill in the gaps.

Michelle: 'Some boys put women down. Most of them think that men should have the best jobs and they should be the heads and all that. They don't seem to realize we have the same potential as they do.'

Joanne: 'They sit there and dish out the orders. They don't feel they've got to help with anything in the house, they think the woman should do all the cleaning, washing the pots and cooking. They expect the woman should look up to them.'

Joanne is resentful, but she admits that boys are more fun, more adventurous and more honest than girls. 'They do more.'

Beverly sits watching the telly, while her brother roams the streets till all hours. Boys are hooked on football, boys are dead serious about music. Boys don't argue over anything special like girls do. They fight for *fun*! 'My brother has fights with his friends and they nearly kill each other. They call it fun.' Mystifying.

Joanne bears the brunt of Chris's social clumsiness. She feels as though he's 'making fun of her', that she 'can't have a serious talk with him', but she still gets a thrill from watching him 'act big'. 'Boys like to boast a lot – they get people coming up to them saying "Have you rumped her yet?" Really stupid.' She knows he's out for what he can get but she fears he will drop her if he gets it. 'It isn't all sweet, the way it is in *My Guy*.' Against this chequered background, boys and girls launch into serious dating. Jackie meets 'Clint Eastwood', and off they struggle into the sunset.

First date

Chris spots Joanne a month later at the school disco. He asks her to dance. Afterwards they turn their back on the giggling gang and choose a table for themselves. Earnestly they discuss the relative merits of 'Judas Priest' and 'Scorpions'. They decide that Blondie is only for little kids these days, almost as bad as Abba! Chris explains some of the finer details of Heavy Rock. But what is really going on in Chris's mind?

75

'You start talking to the girl, and you're really shy, before you're really going out with her, and she's really shy. You're wondering if she's going to say "No" if you ask her out, and that really worries you. You have to be sure that she likes you before you ask her out, otherwise she might say "You must be joking". I mean sometimes they laugh in your face, and you go bright red and try to hide your face under your jacket. You can tell by what she says to you. If she's really nice to you, then she says she likes you. You won't ask her out until then.'

But Joanne does like him, so he nerves up and asks her to go to the pictures with him next week. She is thrilled and terrified. They decide to go and see *Life of Brian*. Chris would have preferred to see *Star Wars*, and Joanne fancied a re-run of *Love Story*, but it is their first date and they both rush to compromise.

On the evening of the date, Chris puts a lot of time into preparing. 'I have a shave first, have a shower, you make sure you're dressed for the part. Then I put clean clothes on as well. I wouldn't put clothes on that I've worn a couple of days before. I'd put proper shoes on, I wouldn't just wear trainers. That's casual isn't it?' Chris carefully puts on deodorant, under his arms and into his shoes. Unlike his father before him, he doesn't want to risk smelling! Joanne, as usual, is agonizing about how much make-up she should wear. Finally they meet. They negotiate their first kiss, the evening is a success and they start going out regularly.

In the gospel according to *Love Story* and *My Guy*, love affairs abound with 'flowers', 'restaurants' and 'diamond rings'. 'Romance is the same as love isn't it, in a way? It's just a posher way of pronouncing it. You imagine a beautiful sunset and a peaceful blue sea.' 'You go to a restaurant, he proposes, floods of tears.' 'They seem madly in love with each other and they never seem as if they'll change their minds!'

Wistful, but pessimistic, Joanne puts romance to one side: 'You get a lot of younger kids reading *My Guy* because they want to know about life. But it's completely different and they get upset when they realize.'

Dating is sweet all the same. She and Chris can't afford to go to the pictures all the time, even when she pays half, so they go for long walks instead. Once over the first embarrassment, they find they can talk to each other. Sometimes they go fishing or shopping, often they go back to his mum's house, and watch television, but they avoid his dad like the plague. 'He takes the mickey all the time. He tells her horrible things about me. She knows it's all lies of course but . . .'

In the gospel according to Men Only, television is not the only means of entertainment open to a boy and a girl. 'Some girls are just looking to go to bed, and that's the best. But if you're going out steady with a girl, you don't go to bed straight away, you leave it until it happens.' Chris is biding his time, but sooner rather than later, he wants Joanne to go to bed with him. This is how he likes to imagine it: 'You have to say a few things, like "I like your body" sort of stuff, and you have a few drinks in a pub. She'll say, "I can't go home tonight, 'cause I've had a row with my mum." So you give her a place to stay for the night. You say, "You can stay at my house – bed and breakfast!"'

Body changes
Chris might be self-conscious that he isn't too tall, he doesn't have a proper beard or his voice hasn't broken yet, but he's not embarrassed about 'scoring' – at least he's not letting on if he is. The urge is strong. But consider the way Joanne feels about her body. She is proud of having enough to fill a bra, but she dreads a boy 'twanging' it at school. It is only eighteen months since she first started her periods, and she is desperately embarrassed about them.

You only have to listen to Sarah and Beverly talking to see how traumatic it is:

'It's horrible, often if you're at school and you get pains, you wouldn't be allowed to go to the toilet in the middle. If you've got a man teacher, what if he won't let you go?' 'Just say, "Let me go". Just go out. You've got to, haven't you?'

'It was a shock when it first happened. I felt ill. I felt about two stone heavier.'

'I wish it had never happened.'

'I seemed to be late in starting, you wondered if your friends were talking about it and wondered if you would be left out. Something wrong with you.'

At thirteen, Beverly dreads going into the showers at school because there's a hole in the wall and the boys all crowd round looking. 'They're there gawking at you as though you're invisible, you know, watching you, and you think "Oh Gawd" and you feel shabby, and that's what embarrasses me.' Look at the lengths one of her friends goes to, to avoid it : 'She's started her periods and she just wraps her towel around her gym kit and sticks her feet under and says, "Oh, miss, I've been in, can't you see my feet are wet?" '

Beverly checks in the mirror after every bath 'to see how her figure's coming along'. She is fascinated and uneasy when she spots the first pubic hair. 'I only noticed about three months ago. I just happened to look in the glass and I saw ... I think they curl.'

Back to Joanne. At fourteen, she is embarrassed about her body, gloomily resigned to her periods and reluctant to be seen naked by anybody. 'My mum's got a boyfriend, and sometimes he would come in and I'd feel a bit embarrassed. Now I won't let no one in the bathroom.' She won't even come out of a dark corner of the disco if she's looking too sexy. Imagine how she feels having to strip in front of a *boy* – imagine how she feels seeing *him* naked! The whole thing is horribly embarrassing.

And what does she know about sex anyway? It's not the sort of thing *Jackie* or *Woman's Own* discuss in detail, she can't ask Mum how to do it, and sex education at school is embarrassing and irrelevant. Why doesn't anybody talk about it openly. Does it hurt? 'I said to my Mum, "Well, what's it like?" "Well, it hurts a bit at first." I says, "If it hurts, why do you do it Mum?" She goes, "Because it shows something to a boy." She's read terrible things in the papers – incest, rape, sex change – she saw a flasher once in the park which upset her dreadfully ...'

What's more, she knows she's going to be assessed on her performance. Not only does she have to do it when she's not sure she wants to, but she's got to do it well. And she doesn't even know if she's doing it right. She reaches out for limits. 'The age of consent is sixteen isn't it? If it wasn't important, they wouldn't have made the law, would they?'

Entering the fray

At sixteen, the agony abates. Michelle can't go on saying 'no' for ever: 'You have said "no" to him once or twice, but you've got to the stage where you're ready to pull your hair out unless you say "yes". I think you want to see if they're going to go out with you even if you don't, before you do, because a lot of boys are out for what they can get anyway. So I think if you say "no" a couple of times ... I think it's terrible to have it off after a few weeks, but if you've been going out with him for a long time ... Some girls that I know have done it loads of times. It's just part of their life.'

She's doubtful, but decided; enjoyment is a side issue. 'It's something new, something that you just want to experience. But then again there's a lot of pressure in it as well'. 'Having it off' for the first time is a very big event. Harry and Andy would brag to their mates until they got beaten up for being boring, but Michelle only tells a chosen few. She's not sure if she wants people to know she's the type.

'I can't imagine telling.'

'They do.'

'But that's gossip between friends.'

'But it gets round the school, like "Debbie had it off last night" and it goes on and on and on.'

'We keep it between the four walls – nobody else.'

The discussion moves on to pregnancy.

In the last year, a surprising number of Michelle's friends have got pregnant, and not the ones you'd have thought either. 'She's always been nice really. I'd never have thought of her doing anything like that. Suddenly now it's people I know. It's just that any girl could get pregnant.'

Bravado invades the discussion.

'It's becoming fashionable to say you think you're pregnant now.'

'Some people do it just to go against the law.'

But underneath, getting pregnant is a serious matter.

'It's not something you want to joke about. I'll do anything so I won't get pregnant. I'll try anything.'

According to Michelle, all the girls in her class know about contraception. Why then do they get pregnant? It is tied up with their ambivalence about having sex in the first place. They don't admit to themselves that they're doing it, and of course if they're not really doing it they can't get pregnant. 'Some girls probably just think, "Oh, I won't get pregnant – there's no point."'

Real maturity comes in accepting responsibility, facing up to the embarrassment of going to the clinic and putting yourself on the Pill. Once you have, the relief is overwhelming. This is how Michelle describes it:

'It's really easy to go on the Pill, but other girls get embarrassed about things like this. They won't bother to go to the clinic, so they'll go with their bloke, get pregnant and then start worrying. But you want to do all the worrying beforehand, before you even think about it. Now it's just like a normal thing to say "I've been up to the clinic to go on the Pill." You don't feel the way you used to. Shock, panic, despair. But now it's "Oh you're on the Pill – great. Join the club."'

All this talk about pregnancy, sex, and scoring, 'Should I or shouldn't I?' 'Will she or won't she?' and not much talk about affection. It is all so fraught.

But they expect things to get better.

After the first rush of dating and trying to score, things slacken off a bit. Chris and Joanne retreat into the company of their friends for a while until they're ready to try again.

Chris: 'I packed her in, I dunno why. I just lost interest. I go round with my mates.'

Joanne: 'Not together all the time. You've got to see other friends. Always people when they meet boys, they just forget about their friends.'

Settling in

As they get older they expect the relationships to grow deeper. Michelle finds that older boys understand her better and she's more open. Harry (sixteen) realizes that girls have personalities too. Everyone expects to get married sooner or later – mostly later.

Harry resolves to have fun first. He's not going to settle down before he's thirty, and when he does he's not going to tell the girl he's got money because 'if she knows you're rich, you'd never know how she feels about you'. The ideal wife has a good personality, nice body, nice features and most important of all 'she likes you'.

The girls have thought more about it, and Michelle and her friends are facing up to the real issues. They enjoy dating and worry that they might be bored settling down with one man.

'Five months is as long as I've ever been out with anybody and that was enough for me.'

'What I want is children. I don't think I'd be able to live with a man without children.'

'You need other obstacles to keep you going otherwise I'd definitely get bored with him. You need another thing to sort of play with, it's like having a dog.'

Me: 'You mean having a child?'

'Yeah. I read in the newspaper the other day that having animals in the house really does calm you down ...'

'Well, I've got about ten gerbils in my room!'

No one agrees with tying themselves down too early.

'Early marriages never last, my sister is seventeen and she's ready to settle down and get married. She's a lunatic.'

The answer is to live with a few blokes first. 'Living with someone and marriage is the same thing except you just haven't got a ring on your finger to tie you down. When we're ready to have children, then I want to marry.'

'My idea of living is keeping up a social life. I want to live with, say, six people.'

Life is alluring as it is, but you can't really go off in a gang of girls if you're married. And if your husband's got friends and you don't like them, it's hard to say, 'Well don't ask them up here.' You have to put up with it. Marrying seems to mean putting up with your husband's friends, giving up outings with the girls, looking after babies and doing the housework.

But attitudes are shifting. Joanne and Michelle have only

just been pressurized into doing the housework at home and they're still resentful. When they are actually faced with having to get up and wash the pots, while their brothers just sit there watching telly, they burn at the injustice. The further removed they are from childhood, the more hotly they defend equality for women. They don't just accept that they should sit at home and cook and clean any more. There's more to life. Says Michelle: 'Marriage – you always regret it and have to do all the housework. I don't want to be like my mum. I don't relish the idea. I'd really like to make a go of a career first!'

In theory at least, the boys aren't against a more equal division of labour, although they may start seeing problems when their future wives hand them the Hoover in the middle of 'Match of the Day'. But already they are taking cookery classes at school and expecting that their wives will work and get well paid for it.

Dating, then, is a slow lead-in to marriage, and the slower the better because dating is fun and divorce is dreadful. The words of the song offer a warning everyone seems to have heeded.

You done too much
Much too young
You're married with a kid
When you should be having fun
Now you're chained to the kitchen
Making currant buns for tea
Ain't you heard about contraception?
Ain't you heard about sterilization?

What does it mean, then, that the average girl gets married at the age of twenty-one?

6 The public face

Adolescence is the first time the young begin to experiment with their image. They begin to think about their public face and get concerned about the way they look. It's easy to play around with image because you can just change your clothes, make-up, hairstyle, follow a new band and buy their records. There are plenty of models to choose from – singers, actors and actresses, personalities, sportsmen and women, friends, adults – you decide what to follow and when to switch. But what you don't do when you're fourteen is experiment on your own; you do it in safety, together with a group of kids just like you.

'Grown-ups aren't anything are they, it's only teenagers who are fashionable.'

Fashion matters – 'I won't go out unless I'm in fashion, if I did they'd laugh at me' – but parents will never understand. 'My mum says: "When you're in my home you do what I say and you get what I say," "I don't care, but you're not coming out with me looking like that!"'

Tina says: 'If you've got a really nice boy-friend you feel good ... you know personality isn't everything ... looks *do* mean a lot, especially at this age. Also he has to like the right music, have smart clothes, go to the good concerts ... if you go to a party with him he'll know when a good record has come on, he'll want to dance, to sing it. He'll know it and all the words.' It all matters and the kids take it very seriously.

They love it when adults say 'I don't understand what it's all about, they all look strange to me.' It helps to reinforce that feeling of separateness from grown-ups and the adult world, and to tighten the bond between kids at school. 'You're part of the same world, it's good to be young.'

The young will always be involved and excited by cults

and fashions, but it's only the minority who are obvious. They're at the sharp end, often the opinion leaders, the ones who lead their mates and influence their tastes. They hear the buzz that goes around, notice any changes on the streets, they always know where to go and what's happening and they pick it up and change accordingly. They care passionately about each fashion that emerges but will change allegiances just like that, when it suits them.

Tina and her friends live in London, are always in the forefront of fashion and are sensitive to movements in the whole scene. At the time of writing this they told me: 'It's a bit dead at the moment, nothing's really happening, but it will, we're just waiting for it ... it's really a bit boring now.' But the whole subject of fashion is not boring to the young. Watch a sullen, lethargic group of fourteen-year-olds come to life when you ask them to talk about fashions. They immediately sit up, take notice, become animated and excited as they fall over each other trying to tell you all at once their own personal views and opinions about clothes, music, dancing, concerts etc.

Not all adolescents are so obviously involved with fashions, but that doesn't mean they don't care about it or follow them. They still have heroes and images that they aspire to, it's just they don't have the courage, the money or Mum won't let them. Or they might just be a bit slow and behind the brighter, sharper opinion leaders.

Opting out
'Snobs' are exceptions however.

Me: 'How do you recognize a snob?'

'At school they don't wear anything fashionable ... they talk different ... they don't go out anywhere and stick to their work ... I think it's the way they're brought up. I think they have a more sheltered life. They're not allowed to do things as much as we are.'

I never met a snob, I just heard about them. It seems to have some connection with social class, although the kids themselves were confused about what that meant. Most thought of themselves as working class and they knew that upper-class people 'have a lot of money, a big home and cars, jobs up in London, going round with suitcases'.

Of those who were interviewed, it was the kids from lower working-class homes who associated themselves more closely with fashions and cults and the middle classes who were more inclined to align themselves with 'ordinary people'. Working-class kids were also more inclined to describe themselves as bored, not very good at school and often influenced by what friends think.

To add to the confusion some boys and girls, while not snobs, opted out, like Debbie.

'I want to be normal, I want to be different, but not too different, I'll go for what I want to, I don't want to be like any of them ...' but she didn't want to be an original, or out on a line. 'I'd rather just be in a group and not stand out ...'

Ian was the same; he liked black and navy clothes but he liked his clothes to be functional and: 'I don't want to be flamboyant, I just want to feel free.'

They listened to the music they liked and bought the records, but they did not want to show openly they followed any particular cult – although they did dress in the basic youth 'uniform' of jeans and T-shirts.

It's not just clothes. Fashions and cults involve music, dancing, ways of thinking and talking, or a particular style of behaviour. When Tina described the ideal boy-friend she mentioned all those things that mattered 'like the right music, smart clothes, go to good concerts, know what all the best records are, know all the words and how to dance to it' – generally knowing what's going on and being there. Boys and girls were constantly telling me about the pressure to know what's happening – that's why they listen avidly to the hit parade, so that they know what records are most popular, and they are expected to know all this in the group. 'It's not just the dress, it's the way you are.'

The school arena
School is the setting for the adolescent fashions and cults. School is where they parade their looks, their knowledge, where

they buy and sell clothes and records, where they look, and learn what's going on. Not everyone is at the same stage, of course, which is what makes it more interesting, but kids at school are sharp and alert to each other:

'Fashion even involves school. If you have a hole in your jumper they take the mick out of you, and boys are sarcastic if you wear old clothes ... people say you're only going to school and not a fancy dress ball but you *have* to look good.'

'You have to look smart, then you're not an outcast. If you didn't look right you'd feel really bad and wish you didn't go to school. For example, if all your jeans were in the wash and you only had one pair left and they were flares then you'd stay at home because you don't want to look stupid ... but my dad wouldn't understand that.'

'At school you see the way your friends are dressed and you get a general reaction from the other people. If they like it too, then you go out and buy whatever they're wearing ... those shoes I bought because I liked them, but my friends all liked them too.'

'One boy turns up in something that looks pretty good and the other bloke comes in with it so it catches on, and it can go from school to school.'

'You want new things when you see everybody else is getting something new.'

Some will always be the leaders: 'A girl in our class is a freak, she'll wear a really nice jumper and a funny, baggy pair of trousers, so you like the top and you'll ask her where she got it from and you'll go out and buy it' – but copying has its drawbacks too – 'then everybody else will start asking where she got it, where you got yours and they go out and buy it as well ... I really hate that.'

Debbie, however, was relieved that her school still had uniform, it gave her a let-out from the rat race:

'I prefer school uniform, then there's no competition about what you wear. I think it's not right that people associate with girls just because they wear nice clothes and they're better than others ... the girls who look more glamorous are always talking more to the boys.'

It also meant you could keep your valued clothes for going out:

'If you wear it to school you've got nothing to go out in at night, nothing different and there's a limit to what you can buy. Mind you, once you've had it a bit you can wear it to school.'

But even when there was school uniform there were always some who would adapt it to suit the latest fashion.

There was a lot of pressure from school to conform to a particular cult, particularly in the fourth and fifth years when there was a need for classification.

'I hate it, since I've had this haircut I walk into school and they keep calling me a Skinhead, it doesn't mean that, it's not even a proper skincut.'

'You get kids coming up to you at school saying what *are* you, a Mod, a Skinhead, a Ted, what? And when I say I'm in between then they say, "Oh, you big fairy."'

'Just because I like the music people say I'm a Mod.'

'You can't be different on your own, whatever you're closest to they label you as it.'

Cult following

Although Michelle, who made that last point, was moving away from a close association with cults, most kids need a sense of identification, and there is a pressure to belong, even though they may change as each new movement attracts them.

'They think you're old-fashioned if you only stay with one group all the time ... that's why my mum still likes Cliff Richard.'

'One minute it's all one sort of music and then a year later it's new, different groups and you think you like that better ... it's always changing.'

'You just do it because it's the in thing, because everybody else does it.'

'My brother likes it because he goes round with Lenny Smith, and I don't know why he likes it. He used to be a Punk a couple of months ago, he just goes with the fashion, I think everyone belongs to one group or other.'

'My friend used to wear flares. She was really nice so we told her to change a bit. Now she wears really tight drains, she looks nice. It's alright if you can tell someone nicely.'

'You have to be in fashion when you go to the disco or you feel left out if you're different.'

'You can't be a Mod if your mates aren't.'

As in any sector of our society, when one group feels strongly about its identity it is bound to clash with another group which also cares intensely about its self-image. It is this strong feeling that makes the identity so attractive. Clashes between the various cults take many forms which range from gentle classroom or dinner-table teasing right through to physical aggression and violence. Girls observe it all but manage to keep out of the fights and stick to abuse and taunting. It is usually the boys who have to fight over their identity and prove their manhood. It put Ian off:

'I used to go to discos and I stopped because there was too much violence. It's silly, it all started because of the different clothes and music – Punks, Mods, Heavy Metallers ...'

'It's the Mods and a load of Punks, they always fight, it's like football, you like one team and then you meet another team and they all start fighting.'

'It does scare you, you walk down the road and see a bunch of them together and if you're on your own it scares you, you think, "Oh God, they're going to get me."'

As individuals, the kids I talked to were ordinary, reasonably tolerant teenagers who just wanted to have fun, but it all begins to happen when they get together in a group.

'I've got mates who are Punks and I speak to them but when I'm out with the gang I stick to the Heavy Metal kids – but I do try and keep out of trouble. It all starts with people insulting each other and then ...'

Harry didn't really understand why but he worried it was all getting out of control:

'It's more than the way you dress and the music you listen to, it's not actually the violence but it just seems to have built up to such a pitch that Virgin Records has to have bouncers ... gangs meet there. Most of them are soft – it's just because they're in a gang that they're acting hard and have prescribed enemies.'

Andrew was relieved underneath that his mum put her foot down sometimes; it saved him from getting into trouble he couldn't handle:

'She wouldn't let me near a Crombie because she's seen skinheads wearing them, she wouldn't let me wear a Sham 69 badge in case Teddy Boys beat me up and I get hurt and she won't let me wear my Mod gear to a football match.'

Loyal cult following is to be taken seriously – it is worth fighting over and the analogy to football is used often.

'There's always fights, trying to prove themselves, to see which is the hardest trend. You come to stick up for your cult ... it's like territory in football ... their turf, you try and get them out, prove who's more powerful, like home crowds invading the terraces. At the Round House or the Rainbow all the different ones hang around outside, just watching and taking the mickey out of the music that's played inside. This guy I know actually wears a disguise so he can get past the bouncers and cause trouble. He gets in and shouts out things inside about their music.'

Because you 'always get someone disagreeing', you've 'always got to have the opposite'. Cults are a very well established aspect of teenage life.

The extremes

The violence is the extreme side of cults and fashion and is limited but there are two cults that seem intimately involved in violence and aggression, while being totally opposite in nature – the Punks and Skinheads. Punks are considered out of date, or certainly on their way out, and Skins are seen almost as a lunatic minority. 'It takes a thousand skins to make one brain!' But they are constantly mentioned and seem to have the strongest identities and more developed 'philosophies' than the other fashions that have been around.

Punk started off as a movement by the young against the establishment. It questioned the way the young were treated by the government, the fashion industry, music industry and the media. It found the establishment hypocritical and removed from the society the kids were living in, so it created its own identity which came from the streets, the kids themselves.

They rebelled against the adult society and caused a revolution in the youth 'scene'. Most of the children interviewed were too young to have been involved in the early days of Punk and they really became interested when it was on the wane as a fashion, but the philosophy and feeling has lived on. Philosophy is an adult word though, and the political side of these two cults is superficial and partly to do with the fashion itself: 'Punks are for anarchy, it's all a laugh.' There is a lot of interest in Punk because it is so anti-everything. Some can really identify with it too:

'It's the only thing that's really interesting and different – they fascinate you.'

'They're there to stand out, be outrageous, be noticed, do things you wouldn't normally do.'

'They turned to Punk because everybody was the same, living in the same houses, wearing the same sort of clothes ... Punk was a way of expressing yourself.'

'They fought to be original.'

Sid Vicious was seen as completely looney and over the top, but many kids admired his nerve and outrageousness; he was an anti-hero getting back at everybody, but for most kids the style of dressing and behaviour was much too extreme, particularly for the younger boys and girls:

'I don't like the way they dress, it makes them look unhappy and they get drunk and scare people,' said Beverly, and she was unsure whether she'd have the courage to actually go out with a Punk.

'I'd worry about being talked about and I wouldn't let my mother meet him.'

'They dress like that to attract attention,' which for a self-conscious twelve-year-old like Sarah was too much to cope with.

Despite the extreme appearance of Punks the young did relate to the songs, particularly those that reached the hit parades – they could all safely be closet-punks. They saw Punk or New Wave bands as singing songs about their world, about life as they saw it, they knew exactly what the words meant because they reflected their inner feelings:

'Punk songs always talk about real life stories and what life

91

is like ... they make you want to sing along with it, to sing what they've found out about.'

'It's a way to express yourself because you can't express it yourself. You may not like to speak out loud but you can if you put it into song.'

Aggression, however, was implicit in Punk. The anti-establishment attitude, extreme appearance and behaviour caused reactions. Outsiders were intimidated and scared by their strangeness whereas rival cults saw this as a reason to pick a fight – they were a sitting target in their outlandish clothes.

'When you dress in a certain way you have to learn to expect trouble.'

'They do scare you when you see them.'

'You've got to look hard if you're a Punk.'

'All the Punks meet in one record shop and all the Rockers and Teds will come round from another place and there'll just be a big gang fight.'

'If you're a Punk you can muck about, spit on people's heads, things like that.'

'They wouldn't hurt a fly, but they just look so evil.'

Michelle had picked up one aspect of the Punks she had met: 'Most of them are upper class, with posh accents ... it's because they want to get away from that.'

Mary loved the idea of being a Punk but: 'It's my freckles, I can't be punk with freckles it just wouldn't look right.'

Punks may just look evil but Skinheads were hard: 'They're mean to their mates, punch them in the mouth.' There was seen to be very little philosophy behind the skins: 'You don't like anything, all you do is go round beating everyone up.' Their anti-black attitudes were disliked. They believed in racial equality. Andy and his friends gave me a closer look into the 'political' nature of the Skins:

'They think they're political and say they're for this country and they all join the National Front and get into rucks, some join the anti-Nazi league just so that they can have a punch-up. The British Movement recruit outside football matches, and they join because it's illegal – well I think it is – it's all for the kicks, to get that adrenalin going, to feel wanted, a rebel ... they like TwoTone music.'

Me: 'But that's about blacks and whites together isn't?'

'Yes, well that's the point. Ian's Dad is black and he's joined the British Movement and wears a Swastika ... they hang around with black kids, they only get involved for the kicks, for the fun and the rucks and to be different, they've not got the brains to be political ... it's the bigger men that organize it.'

So physical violence was symbolic: 'They don't like anything, all they do is go round scaring everyone up.'

Kevin felt that many Skinheads were actually aggressive and chose the fashion because it suited their personality: 'A lot of skins have gone Mod now, but they're still the same, they're still really hard. You expect them to do people over.'

Everyone was scared of them, not just because of the way they looked, as with Punks, but because of real aggro.

'Just because you look like a Mod, part of the crowd, you get Skinheads starting on you.'

'They cause all the trouble at football matches.'

The majority

But it was difficult to get a personal insight from the kids we talked to as none of them had ventured as far as true Punk or Skinhead, in fact few school children had. These cults were extremes and only for the most confident and committed, the real extroverts who didn't have Mum or teacher on at them all the time. None of the other fashions or cults that these young people had experienced or knew about, such as Mods, TwoTone, disco, Heavy Metal, etc., involved such commitment or 'quasi' political beliefs. They are based solely on style, clothes, music and dancing.

Many of the kids mentioned are the leaders in their gangs at school, the ones who are always in touch and who the rest of the gang look to for ideas and information. The majority of kids, however, are happy to follow the crowd rather than lead it. They listen to the hit parade and 'Top of the Pops' and are influenced by friends, local discos, shop windows and magazines for choice of styles. Girls, especially younger girls, tend to be dominated my Mum when choosing clothes and make-up. It is frustrating because there is always that continual conflict with Mum worrying that her daughter looks too old, Dad that she looks too sexy and the girl herself wanting to look the same as her friends. But as in Beverly's case, this dispute is often settled by paying for it yourself:

'I've just bought myself some shoes, some high-heeled courts, my mum said she wasn't buying me any but if I wanted them I could buy them myself, so I did. And I wanted a dress with slits up the side and she said I wasn't to buy it because "your Dad'll play merry hell with me for buying it for you", so she said buy it yourself with your own money and take the blame for it – so I did.'

'I wanted a mini-skirt but Mum wouldn't let me wear it.'

Also, many girls like Sarah, who haven't long left primary school, were nervous about fashion. They were unsure of themselves and were happier to stick to a fairly conventional look. 'When you're older you can act different, wear all the clothes you want to, really go with fashion, but now I just ask my friends and wear the same. I go for basic things. I haven't got the nerve to wear anything a bit outrageous.' Mum isn't so bothered about boys unless they want to wear clothes that might get them into trouble – like Skinhead regalia. Boys, however, still get nagged at by Dad to get their hair cut.

Money of course came into all discussions on fashions, and so much depended on how much you could get out of Mum, what your savings were like or how much you earned in your part-time job. 'You scrounge, ponce off everybody else.' Although money is tight, there are symbols the young can use to show what fashions they follow. The most popular are badges, which are cheap, obvious and give a clear indication of what you believe in; hairstyles, and each cult had its own precise haircut; shoes, which are nearly always the first sign of a new fashion and everyone is very conscious of wearing the right style; costume jewellery; and make-up. The latter is mostly for the girls, but it is a cheap way of showing fashion following and trends.

'It's the little things that can make a difference – hair, earrings, make-up.'

'She looks good, she wears pickers and pale tights.'

'Henry he's nice, he wears Beatle boots, pointed ones.'

Getting ideas

But where do they pick up all these fashions, get interested
in the cults, and where do they display them? It's the same
place, it's where there are people like themselves around,
where the young hang out. School of course is important.
They're there every day, talking, messing around, swapping
information and new ideas, buying and selling clothes and
records, reading magazines. Outside school, the streets are
where it all happens. The most fashionable kids are the ones
who are out in the streets most, the ones who live near city
centres, and whose parents have least control or concern about
them. They are always the kids who know what is going on.
Fashion is about display and showing off, and on the streets
you attract the most attention; but it has to be the right
street – Tina knew all about that: 'We wouldn't be left behind.
We're up Oxford Street and Carnaby Street, that's where the
fashion is. On Saturdays everyone goes up there and poses,
they all try and look their best so that's where we go. Everyone looks really smart down there, we wouldn't go down there
if we didn't look good.' And display they did: 'When the Mods
were in, there was this one shop we'd go to, just walk around,
it was all green, an arcade and there were pool tables and one
armed bandits and you'd walk in there and all the mods would
stop what they were doing and look. Then if they thought
you looked good, they'd smile at you and you'd smile at them.
You go there to pose and look good.'

Not all kids are as concerned as Tina and her friends about
posing but they do all get ideas from the street. 'You just see
people, on the street, looking good and if you really like what
they're wearing then you'll go out and buy it.' Shops are on
the street too, so they can look in the windows and get ideas.
They weren't very sure how shops fitted into the teenage
fashion scene.

'Micks in Romford is the best shop around. I don't know

how they find out about it first; it's always in the windows before it comes out anywhere else, or before you see it on the telly – it's always modern stuff.'

'I suppose someone somewhere thinks up these things ... look at the groups on telly I suppose.'

'Clothes manufacturers hear about fashion and make up and advertise their clothes and get the ball rolling after it's started.'

But there is also a move away from the conventional shops, and trendsetters like Michelle and Tina also go round flea markets, antique stalls, secondhand clothes shops looking for original clothes. 'Originality does make a lot of difference. It's much better if you've got something that's original.'

Record shops are another place to be seen and to see what's happening. Because music tends to give birth to fashions and cults, a record shop is the ideal place to be. The young go there to listen to the music and look at the records, generally to get an idea of what's going on in the music scene and what's new. Shops become a sort of daytime club and display ground. These are usually the smaller, independent record shops that specialized in the music the young like, rather than the chain stores that cater for the family. They retain a degree of exclusiveness. But because they attract the cult members they also attract trouble and some record shops have to employ bouncers to keep the peace.

Concerts are seen as the best display ground for fashion because they attract the styles that go with the music – but concert goers have to be careful, as Tina said:

'You dress up to go to a concert, you have to look good because there's loads of other people there. You must wear the right thing though, modern to see a Mod concert like Jam, because if all the other Mods look really smart you're going to be shown up – if you wear the wrong thing you'd get chucked out. If you like different types of music yet only dress in one style, then you can't go. For instance, if you like Madness and want to see them, you've got to dress like a skin or get done in.'

The real problem with concerts though, is that they are expensive and not always easy to get to for those kids who live outside city centres, and many now ban kids under eighteen. Discos are the best place to see what's happening, and most young people go to them. The type of disco varies and while some of the older boys and girls may visit the commercial venues, usually the kids at school go to the local discos in town halls, church halls, youth clubs, over pubs or even those organized at school. It is here they listen to music, dance, dress up and see what everyone else is wearing and meet people. They usually charge a reasonable admission too. It is the main social scene for the majority of this age group. Discos are good fun.

'I like going to them. When you get fed up at home you can go out and really enjoy yourself.'

Twelve-year-old Sarah described her local disco:

'There's coloured lights, but it's all dim and the lights go blue, green and pink on the walls and things.'

Me: 'But what do you like about it?'

'The bright lights, the music, the loudness, the way everyone dances. There are seats around the edge and everyone sits there swinging their legs like this.'

Then Sarah and the other girls went on to show me how they danced and how the boys danced and wanted me to play some music – they loved it. They feel relaxed in the company of other young people. 'We dance in a bunch, we dance with different people, often those we've never seen before, it's good.' But the boys who can't dance just don't go.

The success or failure of a disco largely depends on the music.

'The music is either pop or soul, it really depends on which disco you go to and who runs it. You get a lot of Mods up there and a lot of Soul and sometimes they have fights.'

'The last one was terrible, they kept playing all that Punk music and you can't dance to that.'

Simon hated it when they underestimated him:

'Usually when they have discos for children like us they play rubbish music like Boney M. They should have something like Police and Blondie, that would be much better.'

But clothes matter too.

'I really want some new clothes. You have to be in fashion

when you go to a disco because if you're not they all give you funny looks and you feel left out and different.'

'You look around for a girl to dance with, a nice girl you can talk to, someone who likes a lot of music and is in fashion ... a disco type of girl.'

As they get older though, the girls in particular prefer the town centre discos.

'Basically any disco's the same, the music is blaring out, but I like the more glamorous surroundings of the ones in Manchester; there's more variety of people, whereas the local discos are people you've grown up with. It's more attractive to go to the big discos – you can meet new people.'

But they are not really allowed in to many of them.

'The police are always trying to stop them because kids of fourteen get in. You're supposed to be eighteen.'

If you do get in to the older discos though, you have to behave accordingly.

'There's always bigger kids than you; you can't act hard. If you muck about you get thrown out and banned so there's no point – anyway if you muck about you look childish.'

All the other venues for learning about fashion are less formal and depend on who is there – chip shops, cafés, cinemas, leisure centres, swimming pools, skating rinks, parks, parties – they are wherever the young are ... messing about.

Pubs

Pubs and clubs are a venue, but it depends on how old you look. At fifteen or sixteen most young people have been in a pub and many have had alcoholic drinks. 'Most people of fourteen or fifteen nowadays go and have a pint in the pub.' Once you look old enough to go to them they become another place to meet young people although the fashion element seems to be missing by comparison with the arena of the school or the disco.

What the pub represents though, is a symbol of maturity, of moving away from childish activities. They all know they're not allowed to drink in the pub, and this of course gives it the excitement, particularly for the girls. Michelle and her friends regularly go to pubs with friends, it's one of the few places for young people to go in the evenings, but they are always wary:

'We go to the King's Head. You get a lot of young people of our age there so I feel relaxed in there, you don't have to worry about anything. In other pubs though you have to worry all the time about being caught drinking. The police come in and start checking, and we have to run out then. When you walk in you always get funny looks from the barman. What I really dread happening is that the barman sees you on the other side of the room and shouts. "Oh, look at that little girl over there," and everybody turns round and looks at you.'

Debbie felt as bad: 'You go into pubs to show off, to try and look big, but you're always worried someone will say, "Oh, you're too young to be here, go away." Sometimes when you're in there you feel so little, you feel like everybody is watching you, and you sit in the corner feeling all cramped up, hiding away.'

It was nerve-racking, and that made it all the more fun. 'It's one of those things where you do it just to prove you can, like going to X films. After you've done it, it doesn't matter.' But if the drinking age were lowered it would spoil it. 'It would be just like going to a youth club then, and you'd end up sick of watching adults.'

Boys in particular like the opportunity to mix with older teenagers or adults. It helps them to get to know and understand the adult world and broaden their experiences of life. It also introduces them into an essentially male world that they do not meet at home or at school.

'I like pubs because it's a good place to get away and have a talk and to listen to people. It's good to sit down and talk about the big race. There's more people there than a café and it's more interesting.'

Pubs are an adult world – that is their appeal – but some kids are still self-conscious about intruding. 'A lot of older people don't like a load of kids in there. They go there to get away from it all and they get annoyed to see us hanging around.'

Those who are much too young to go to pubs know all

about them and they are seen as places for socializing and having fun, but pubs do seem to have a very male image.

'They're for beer and friends, to get away from nagging wives.'

'Men go out to the pub and come home late at night and you don't see them very often ... they go there with their friends at work and stay out.'

Even if they don't visit pubs they have all had alcoholic drinks – some occasionally and some regularly – and they all expect to drink when they get older. Drinking is a sign of growing up, it's moving away from childish things, and they start to practise quite early, about the same time they're experimenting with fashion. Three-quarters of the youngest boys and girls who were interviewed, eleven–twelve-year-olds, had tried alcohol. All this early experimentation goes on in the home and with the approval of Mum and Dad.

'I like Bacardi and Coke. I have that at Christmas. First had it when I was eleven; Dad was having some so I tried some of his and then I liked it so I had some myself.'

'My friend's mum had some Martini in and we were drinking it neat; she didn't mind at all ... I got a little bit tipsy.'

'I've had rum and whisky, advocaat. My grandad has given it to me, and I've had it on holiday.'

In some of the more middle-class homes boys like Simon are getting used to wine with their meals. 'I always have wine when they have it. I don't have much. We always have it with Sunday dinner.'

The real drinking, however, goes on away from home or when Mum and Dad are out, with booze they've bought at the off licence.

'I go to parties where we drink once or twice a month. In December every Saturday is a party. When we have discos at school whoever looks oldest nips into the off licence and buys lager.'

'When you drink it makes you feel much happier and you forget too.'

'I went to a party where there were all fifteen- and sixteen-year-olds, and they didn't have any soft drink there; it was all whisky and gin. His mum and dad were out, and we all got pissed.'

Like Kevin, a lot of the older boys and girls could tell me tales about getting drunk – 'Loads of times me mum and dad's been in when I've got drunk, especially at Christmas, but you have to be careful when you're out with all the drunks about. Mum always tells me to be in early.' 'I feel in a real state when I'm pissed. I usually puke up then fall asleep on the nearest thing' – although the more sophisticated girls were not so sure about it – 'I see my friends at parties and they look so stupid. Some of the things they do they really show themselves up; they don't know what they're doing.' I asked boys and girls like Joanne and Kevin why they drank alcohol:

'It gives you a feeling of self importance.'

'It's the effect it has on me. I just like it, I feel alright, I'm able to muck in with everybody else and have a good laugh.'

'It makes you feel good. You don't really know how you feel when you're drunk but you say things you wouldn't say normally – like to a girl you could say you wanted to sleep with her and you wouldn't say it when you're sober ... you can tell her you fancy her a lot. The only trouble is you get into trouble, throwing up, hangovers, getting up in the morning. I was sick on the teacher at school once!'

Sarah has seen why grown-ups drink: 'People drink to get boozed. Some people want to forget things, say they're getting a divorce and they're to trying to get over it, they start heavy smoking and heavy drinking to get over it and then drunks who can't afford it move on to meths.' Kevin thought girls got scared of drink. 'Not many girls drink spirits because they're too frightened to think what they might do if they got drunk.'

What do they actually drink and why? There was quite a difference between the boys and girls in what they drink. Harry is fairly typical of the boys: 'If I'm in a pub and someone else is buying, it's whisky and ginger. I love it although my mum thinks it's a bit strong, but if I'm on my own I drink beer, lager, and when I go to a party I take wine or beer – beer's cheaper because you get quite a lot for a pound.' Joanne spoke for many girls: 'I started drinking shandies or cider, but I like

Pernod on its own and I like brandy ... someone gave me Pernod to try and I thought it was great ... you just try it. When you go to parties and things or on holiday and they say what do you want – I look at everything and try it.'

Generally, boys drank what they were expected to drink as males – beer and lager, particularly strong lagers, and if they drank spirits, it tended to be whisky because it had a 'macho' image. They seemed to start acquiring the taste early on from Dad, who liked to see his son growing up in his own image, and this was encouraged by widespread drinking of shandy. Girls, on the other hand, had a much wider repertoire of drinks which ranged from lagers, cider and shandy through Babycham, wine, sherry and all the drinks that could be mixed with lemonade and Coke. Mixed drinks such as Cinzano and lemonade, Bacardi and Coke, Pernod and blackcurrant, were particularly popular with the girls as they found the soft drink tended to kill the taste of the alcohol, which none of them liked.

Drinking alcohol made the boys and girls feel more grown up; they thought it gave them a degree of sophistication that fashion never could. Also, the advertising for drinks on television and in the cinema was very popular and well remembered. The girls specially loved the glamour of the Martini 'jet set' commercials and they indulged in the fantasies portrayed in them.

In comparison, food had none of these desirable images and adult connotations for the young. Food was just fuel. They were always hungry and always eating. Going out for a romantic dinner was in the future.

Music

But back to fashion, because no matter how young you look, you can follow it.

Music is the basis of most fashions and cults. It reflects what is happening at street level, and that undercurrent of feelings held by the young. It is always changing and evolving, and currently there is a wide range of musical styles to identify with. Each cult has a strong sense of identity with a particular style of music and specific bands and singers. As already mentioned, the live concerts are a good example of the close relationship between clothes and music – you dress up in the right style of clothes to go and hear you favourite band or else you get kicked out. It's practically impossible to separate out the various elements of fashion; they are closely entwined. 'To get a fashion going you'd need music to go with it; you find out a new band, find out their style, find a fashion to go with it and promote the band.'

Boys appear to care more deeply about music than the girls. Although this is a generalization, girls seem more interested in all the outward signs of fashion – playing the right records, dancing to them, hero-worshipping the idols, wearing the right clothes. The boys talked at much greater length, depth and seriousness about the skill and expertise of the various musicians and what bands they had played for in the past. They seemed more interested in the technical side of music, learning about the band and in aspiring to play or sing like that.

I tried to find out where the fashions in music came from and how the news travelled around, but it didn't work like that. Andy astutely described the evolution of musical tastes as being like a tree, continually spreading out its branches with new ones springing up all the time.

The word gets round about new records or musicians in a number of ways. Live apearances in pubs or concerts often start off a following, but the trouble is that many of these places prohibit children under sixteen to eighteen years of age because of the drinking and fighting. But often friends or older brothers and sisters have been at the concert and they tell you all about it.

The radio is a very good source of what is happening at the grass roots level, but these programmes are the late night, eso-teric shows such as John Peel, who makes a point of finding out about new bands and giving them a live slot or playing a record. There are also late-night pirate radio stations that play the more basic, non-commercial records distributed by small record labels. There is a lot of status involved in these inde-pendent record labels; they are for real enthusiasts, those who really know what is happening at the grass roots. 'You'd never hear them on "Top of the Pops"!' Specialist or independent record shops often stock the newest records and they can be listened to there. 'You hear a group on the radio, just one song maybe, you like it, and then go to a record shop and get it.' Once you are interested in a particular style of music then the enthusiastic watches out in the record press for any reports of their gigs or news of what they are doing, and pictures that they publish.

Loyalty

Music did seem to fall into narrow categories or styles that were associated with the cults, and if you followed that cult you also had to openly admire the music. 'You have to be loyal; if you follow one style you are almost forced to like the music and you have to tell your mates you like it.'

'I like Mod music, at least you can tap your feet to it ... no, it's rubbish, when you're listening to AC/DC or Heavy Rock, you can freak out, do a bit of head banging. You've got to admit that's better than tapping your feet ... do you really enjoy tapping your feet?'

Faith, belief and loyalty to a cult was prevalent amongst the more fashionable boys. They couldn't explain it – they didn't really understand it themselves, so how could they tell me what it all meant. Andy tried to explain using the example of 'Soul Boys': 'Soul is probably the most hated cult, it's always slightly off all the fashions. Those of us who believe in our fashions get annoyed by that; they're only doing it purely for the looks, the fashion itself, they're posers. If you really like something you *follow* it ... oh I can't explain.' Tina also hated posers: 'A poser might dress Mod and then they might wear baggy trousers, or one week they're Mod, then Skin comes in so they are Skin, then they decide Punk is smart. They'll say "I know it's not in at the moment but I like it," so they'll turn Punk.'

Perhaps it's the reaction against the violent narrow followings of some cults but things seem to be changing slightly to the informed and the confident –

'If you're truthful you face up to liking the music you like regardless of whether your friends do.'

'It's better to be open, to have mixed fashions, to go with what you want.'

'Now it's getting to be fashionable to be open-minded, it seems to be slowing down.'

But the continual problem is 'You can't be different on your own, and whatever you're closest to they still label you as it.' Maybe having such a range of cults has spoilt them for choice.

'Music now is boring, plain, all singing about love – stupid, or else all the words are the same.'

'Every fashion's been done now. There's not much left to do ... look back, most fashions come out, die out and re-appear twelve years later.'

'None of the music that comes out will be any good for tomorrow; things from the past are just much better.'

Nostalgia

There was always a hint of nostalgia around. Many of the young had this feeling that everything had been better in the past. 'Mods now and then are so different. In the sixties it wasn't violent, it was peaceful then, it was only about the clothes.' They also don't have much idea of the timespan involved and it all got telescoped. 'It was peaceful then because of the hippies, they were going round loving everybody.'

It's amusing to see parents held up as heroes because of their past youth:

'My mum had green and brown pickers; she wore green pickers on her wedding day. Everyone took the piss out of her, so she threw them in the dustbin a couple of years later. I was looking all through the house for them, I wish she'd kept them.'

'Pink Floyd have been going for fifty years and they've only just had a Number 1 in the hit parade. My mum's got some of their old records.'

But whatever their past, they were still parents. 'My mum won't let me have a mini skirt. It's not fair – she used to wear one when she was young but she still says no!'

Heroes

Mum and Dad as they are now will never be heroes to the young, so who are the heroes of the young, who do they admire and who would they like to look like? The answers range from the man-next-door, a girl at school with nice hair through to Clint Eastwood and Debbie Harry. It changes with fashion and trends, it's never static and these are times when you don't really want to look like anyone, or you like the way you look now. Almost one in five of the boys and girls we interviewed felt that way!

Boys identify more with musicians than any other type of person, and they are three times more popular than sportsmen. Girls seem to prefer actresses or filmstars to those in music, but Debbie Harry was by far the most popular single heroine, followed by Olivia Newton John. They thought Debbie Harry was pretty and they loved her records, but despite being favourite they found her clothes too extreme for them to copy. 'I love the music, but she looks a mess.' 'She's nice, you couldn't ignore her, she turns heads, but she wears strange clothes.' Girls went much more for looks and appearance than boys. They had a long list of TV personalities that they admired for their prettiness and the clothes they wore. 'You look at the television, see how they're dressed, and that's what appeals to you.' The only heroes that stood out for the boys were Clint Eastwood, Kevin Keegan and The Fonz. Clint Eastwood was admired for a combination of his good looks and the very 'macho' image he portrayed on screen, all those cowboy and Dirty Harry detective types. 'He's everybody's hero, he's hard, predictable and tough.' It's not surprising he was so popular with the boys who were struggling to prove their manliness. Kevin Keegan of course was the superstar footballer, every schoolboy's dream. The Fonz was funny, but the popular anti-hero type admired by the young.

Moving on

Generally, following fashions and cults is most fervent when you're an adolescent. 'It's fun, gets you excited, it's something to do, you can get involved in the lyrics, the music, the fashion.' Talk to a fourteen-year-old boy or girl about fashion and you'll see how much it means to them. But adolescence is only a stage, kids grow out of it, usually when they are going into pubs regularly and mixing with adults and older teenagers and when they start thinking about jobs or university. Then the slavish automatic following of fashions begins to wane too. Listening to Michelle talk about her opinions on life it was clear that at sixteen she was gradually maturing into that next stage. Her views about fashion were changing too. A little while ago she was a Punk, now ... 'Most of them do it 'cause it's the thing, 'cause everybody does it ... but I'm getting into myself, I want to get into what I want, not what everyone else does ... as long as it's comfortable I'm OK, I don't care what I look like, I'm wandering about now in these, they're falling apart but I like them and everybody takes the mickey out of me.' These, however, were a very tight pair of jeans that were carefully contrived in the way they were 'falling apart'.

Tina had noticed this change in her friend's older sister. 'When she was at school she was just like one of us but now she's ... I don't know, she wears high-heeled shoes, and she looks much older and acts older ... it's the way she takes everything, she goes round with older people. Now she'll go to pubs, she dresses different, she's more grown up mentally too, more settled now she's seventeen.'

Most kids, while they're still adolescent, still at school, are happy to follow the crowd. They want to be like their friends, to support different cults, to become totally involved in the clothes, music and dancing. They want the freedom to switch around, move with the trends. Grown-ups always tell them they all look alike, but that's not true, it's just that adults don't see the subtle differences, they don't understand. But who cares what adults think, their fashions are for the middle-aged, they should stick to Marks & Spencer where they belong. Kids are happy the way it is, they know how it works, they know where to go and how to find out what's happening. They love it out on the streets, they feel at home, they're with other people like them, they're all young and enjoying themselves, just messing about in their own world. It's not for us to intrude, just to leave them alone and accept them.

7 The private face

Me: 'Aren't I keeping you, haven't you got plans for this afternoon? Tell me if you want to go.'

Tina: 'No, we've got nothing to do, we can never think of what to do, we spend all our time going round to each other's houses talking about what we could do but we never know what to do, there isn't anything, it's boring ... I rang up the radio once, they have these schemes for holidays and I asked what suggestions they had for where we could go but when I told them I was fourteen they said I was too old. That's the trouble – you're either too old or it costs too much. Six weeks is much too long, you get really bored in the holidays.'

Tina and her friends were certainly bored and fed up with their spare time during the day, they were looking for a bit of excitement. After that session I gave them some money for lunch but I later found out they had used it to buy a bottle of gin and vodka and they had brightened up their afternoon by getting drunk. But it was a dilemma trying to keep them from boredom ... they all wanted to be out doing things, being active.

Holiday boredom

Harry and his mates knew what Tina meant: 'We just spend our time walking around, looking for something to do, there aren't enough things going on, we don't have any youth clubs and anyway that's only for an hour.' Harry talked for all kids: 'It's boring round here ... but it is everywhere, I've got mates all over and they say the same ... nowhere to go ... you're either stuck in the house or messing about on the street.'

Michelle agreed: 'There's not much to do ... the common up one end, the park down the other, we're in between two shopping places, there's nowhere to go in the evening, only the pubs.' But she was lucky she looked old enough to drink in pubs.

Kenny had always been tall for his age so he had been going into pubs since he was fourteen, two years ago. He found the adult company and all the chat more stimulating: 'I like talking to older people. They talk about sports, joking, politics, the Russians conquering Europe in twenty-four hours, arguing. I like watching them argue, I don't like boring people who don't say anything.'

Some of the lessons might be boring but school itself wasn't:

'A couple of weeks of holiday is fun but after that it gets boring ... I miss my school friends and my little sister always ends up crying and Mum keeps saying, "Why don't you play with your sister?" It's just not the same with sisters or cousins.'

'I get bored in the holidays, you're sitting there outside, your friends have gone out and you've got no one to go out with so you sit there all by yourself.'

Activities were not always enough in themselves, they needed something extra, or a longer enjoyment span.

'This guy over the road spends all that time making models; he hangs them up and then when he gets bored he'd get his Lego out, makes a catapult and breaks them all up by shooting them down.'

'I used to play Japs and Commandoes; we used little guns and used to go round killing everybody, but it was pretty boring when you'd shot everyone ... I used to play with Lego too, building things, but I don't do that now either, I find more interesting things to do.'

'Ballet, museums, art galleries things like that are boring, they're all the same ... I prefer the ones like they've got in Manchester with all the engines that are working. I don't like the zoo much either, you're not doing anything.'

The bored mind conjured up all kinds of schemes, as Beverly described: 'In a friend's garden we get a box, tilt it, leave a trail of bread going into the box and then get some wire and tie it on and thread it through the window. When a bird comes up to peck the bread you get the box over it; it's caught and you can examine it and let it go.'

Me: 'Oh, are you interested in birds?'

'No, not at all, we just do it for fun, something to do.'

Even telly could lose its excitement sometimes, like on a Saturday afternoon: 'If I don't go to football I watch the telly continuously from nine-thirty but there's too much horse racing on. I don't like that – I get bored. Last week I ended up reading.'

A place to go

Excitement was being active, doing things, being involved. They don't have any money but teenagers do have energy. Tina and Harry are fourth and fifth year at school, but they've never met. Tina lives on a typical 1950s council estate in London and Harry on a large, modern, private estate in the suburbs of Leeds. Both they and their friends, however, wanted the same thing: 'I wish there was somewhere we could go that was ours, I wish there was an old house that the council could give us and then we could do it up and call it our own and have all our friends there.' 'We want a place we could go, just one big place where we could meet our friends and meet other people, our own place.' Sometimes they find 'private' places. Tina and Janet had managed to get the key to a boarded up, abandoned house, whereas Andrew and his friends hung about on roof-tops, old air-raid shelters or dumps. As well as being their own, there was also the added excitement of being found out by the police and warned off.

This age group knew about youth clubs and they some-times visited them but they weren't right, they weren't what they wanted, they found them too organized, there were rules and they did not feel free or in control of the situation. 'A youth club is a place to go if you want to keep dry, but you have to do what other kids tell you and that gets on my nerves.' 'In a way youth clubs are too well organized. They are trying to fit people in just so they can make friends. They don't let you get on with it yourself. They push you into it – that's what I find.' Some of the younger kids liked the organi-zation, but although someone like Michelle quite enjoyed the odd visit to her youth club she preferred the freer atmosphere of a local disco: 'A youth club is somewhere to go, everybody knows everybody else and you can have a game of pool

110

together ... but if you're new you get dirty looks, you have to know everybody from the start ... I prefer a disco. There's a good one at the Town Hall, it's really good, everyone's friendly, but then it's run by seventeen and nineteen-year-old people and they've made it really good because they know what they like ... adults wouldn't know.'

The young people I talked with, especially the girls, were always telling me how much they enjoyed being with their best friends. They enjoyed it best when their parents or brothers and sisters weren't around. It became their own special time that they could share with those they felt close to. It seemed to be a sign of the first steps towards building relationships outside the family. 'It's not the same with sisters and cousins – they're not the same as your friends.'

Having friends stay the night was very popular: 'We stay up late and watch the horror films and talk and natter before we go to sleep and then we don't go to sleep until about five a.m. ... in the dark we talk about the things we've done during the day, arguments we've had at school, people we dislike and who we both like,' 'I love it when my friend Sarah comes round to stay. We play around on my bed, do acrobatic rolls and things and we fight. It's all great fun. She shows me how she fights at school and what to do.'

Even just watching the television or playing records was better when parents are out: 'When you have friends round, we just sit there, watch telly, listen to records ... it just feels so much freer when they're all out.' 'Just enjoy it with your friends, you have a laugh, do what you want to do.' 'We go round to each other's houses and watch the horror films; it's good because when you're with your friends you can be really silly, take the piss out of what they're doing, have a laugh, but when my dad's there he's always telling me to shut up and be quiet.' Parents put the damper on everything but younger sisters and brothers are a real pain. 'My sister always wants to come in when we're playing ... we won't let her, we lock the door, and then she goes off crying to my mum and she keeps saying, "Why don't you play with your sister?" She just doesn't understand.'

My bedroom

Whether you're on your own or have friends round, your bedroom is a very special place – your own territory. 'It's private, friends can come in and you can tell your sister to get out.' Sarah loved having her own bedroom and described it to me: 'Everything there is yours, everything you want is in it. You don't have to share it with anybody else ... you can play music, throw books there, bits and bobs, worthless things really but they're worth something to me. They're things given to me by special people, things like Valentine cards, a big metal car, posters, some framed pictures ... I go there if I'm depressed. I can do just what I like without anybody else bothering me.' Privacy is difficult to obtain in a family so maybe that's why it's so highly prized and so bitterly fought for by adolescents. Michelle made a vehement protest to me about her mum intruding into her bedroom. Her mum had found some contraceptives and was creating about it. Michelle was not indignant about the accusations or the fact that they belonged to her brother but because her mother had trespassed and she resented it.

Home itself was OK, it's just the interference the young don't like. Home could be a haven sometimes because 'outside' there was the constant pressure to keep up with the group, to do all the right things and wear the right clothes etc. Sarah enjoyed being with the gang at school but sometimes she liked a break ... 'I'm most at ease at home, I feel I can do and say as I like ... I don't like it best but I feel at ease from that point of view, I don't feel scared to do things.' Ian was very conscious of what his friends might say if he let on to them. 'I've got hundreds of soldiers that I never play with now ... I'd be called childish or something ... but I do sometimes play with them but I don't tell anybody ... you won't tell them ... if they found out I'd be called a baby ... electric trains are all right, they're more technical and actually work, but I couldn't be seen just pushing a train around.' Sarah was a bit self-conscious about her dolls too: 'I still love my dolls, I take them up to my cousins to play ... but ... it's better to play with people, it's more realistic. I go out with my friend and her little brother of about a year, I like to take him out for a walk, it's better fun than dolls.'

Hobbies

It was the older kids who were most vocal about boredom, who found it difficult to fill in that space between school and going out; they felt trapped: 'We're either too young or too old but whatever we are we're the wrong age.' Again lack of money was one of the main problems but some got over this by their part-time jobs which filled in the time and gave them that welcome extra money. Others had to spend much of their time on homework because exams were looming ahead. But most of them were like Andrew: 'It's usually pubs at week-ends, during the week hanging about the bus stop or the chip shop. There may be a party and some nights we might play football,' and as they got older and had more of a life outside home, television began to lose much of its glamour, unless you watched it with your mates. 'I'm never at home but if I am I go to my room and listen to records or music on the radio, I don't like the TV, there's my mum and my kid brother and sister watching it.'

This aimless, restless feeling was not there in the younger kids. They spent more time at home but seemed content and able to occupy themselves in that in between space. They watched a lot of television but also found time for their hobbies and passion for collecting things which was as strong as ever. They collected stamps, postcards, beer mats, belt buckles, toy cars, trains and records. The 'bazaar' nature of the school playground made it an ideal place for swapping, selling and showing off collections. The recent interest in 1960 records even turned some boys into playground entrepreneurs who dealt in old records. The boys were unable to say why they collected things: 'I collect postcards, ones with maps on, I don't know why,' but it seems that it is acquiring the collection itself that has the appeal rather than the things that are being collected. Model making was very popular with the boys; it was constructive and they could see what they had achieved, but the models they made were still the same traditional cars,

113

planes and ships. The more exciting constructions however were the adult type that linked in with the science lessons at school: 'I got an electrical kit for Christmas, and it's smashing. I can make a lie detector, morse code tappers and even a type of radio.' Simon was crazy about Hot Rods and he used the Custom Car magazines to give him ideas about how to give his model cars fancy paintwork. Although by about fourteen or so the boys had grown out of model making, some boys continued their practical hobbies but preferred to give it a more serious, adult air: 'Someone gave me an old radio and I messed about with it and fixed it; now it's my own personal hobby and I've got lots of radio sets.' 'A neighbour got me interested in photography ... I now really enjoy it.' But what seems highly relevant is that these activities had nothing to do with school. Usually they were solitary – done on rainy Saturday afternoons, during the holidays or if they got bored with telly. It was the formal groups like the Scouts and Guides that made hobbies a shared activity and then they were usually on a bigger scale too: 'We design and make go-carts, and they can go as fast as twenty mph.' Board games were not solitary and needed more than one player but that could be a problem at home: 'I've got some good games, but the trouble is my little brother don't like losing and he always loses and then gets argumentative and cries; then I sit and laugh at him.'

A big restriction for the younger boy and girl was the dark nights. They hated winter because it was usually dark when they got home from school so they had to stay in, they weren't allowed out to play.

Partly because of this and partly a sign of the times was the increasing popularity of the electronic games that could be played on the TV.

Activities

Overall, amongst the younger adolescents, there was a very wide range of interests, but they would often flit around between the various activities, and much depended on their circumstances; where they lived; how much money they were given to spend; what their natural talents were etc. Those who had the talent loved to draw or to doodle; girls who lived near the country tended to go horse riding, those who had a good sports centre nearby might take up squash. Sports centres were popular because they provided a wide variety of activities, but the trouble with many such organized games was the cost. Pocket money was unlikely to stretch to going swimming or ice skating every day, especially at some of the new centres 'It's not fair; they charge the same for a child as they do for an adult.'

Football was universally popular with the boys and could be played in a local park – but what could also get boring unless you were aiming to play for a professional team. Sports facilities, though weren't the answer to what to do with your spare time. 'I think adults say "Oh, there's swimming pools near by or there's ice skating," but no one wants to go there *all* the time, every evening, all the evening, and what do we do with swimming pools in the winter?'

Cycling was very popular and its appeal lay in being a cheap way to travel around. It gave them access to a wider area – they could cycle to the next town or out into the country – it added a degree of freedom. But, as with most things outside home, the boys and girls tended to do it in a group, with friends.

Food

There was another way to fill up the space between school and going out – by eating. Simon walks in the door, throws his school bags down, switches the telly on and goes into the kitchen to make himself something to eat and drink. He puts the kettle on for the coffee and then starts poking around; he goes to the biscuit tin and starts munching, looks in the freezer, but can't be bothered to wait for the individual pizzas to defrost and for the oven to heat up, so he puts some toast under the grill and then thinks about whether to make some scrambled eggs or to open the tin of baked beans.

His mum is at work so he has the house to himself for another hour and he'll settle in front of the telly to eat his snack. He enjoys cooking:

'When I cook I open a tin ... Yes, it's not exactly hard is it, but I'll never wash-up, Mum can do that.'

Andrew was the same: 'I know how to cook frozen snacks – pizzas – take them out of the freezer and put them under the grill.'

On Sunday afternoons Beverly made the cake for tea and when her mum was in hospital she helped her dad make the Sunday roast. But Ian was just as good at making cakes, he had learnt how to at school. Andrew would have his mates over for lunch during the holidays but he would rely on the freezer to provide the chips, beefburgers and the cheesecake to follow.

Convenience foods are a boon for today's adolescents because they're always in a hurry, rushing about, out to football practice, round to friends' houses to play records, off to the riding lesson, out messing about on a bike, watching 'Grange Hill' on the TV. Food was great, they were always hungry but never had the time to eat, so the quicker and easier to prepare the better. 'I come in hungry and I want something ready as I'll be going out straight away.'

They were interested in the new food technology and the introduction of the pot noodle snacks could have been made specially for them:

'Isn't it clever, the way you just put the water in the pot and all the meat is cooked, marvellous, they taste good too.'

'I like the curry ones.'

'I come home, Mum's still at work, just take it out, put the water in and stir and it's something hot to eat.'

The other good thing about convenience foods was that you couldn't make a mistake – foolproof, perfect results every time, unless you were so busy rushing about that you forgot to turn the fishfingers over and they got burnt.

These days boys are just as likely to cook as girls: 'I'm a good cook, I can make bacon and eggs and cakes, but I don't do much because Mum does it all.' But food doesn't have the glamour or status of a beer, whisky or martini and lemonade. However, no one is going to doubt your manhood if they see you making your own spaghetti on toast, you don't have to apologize to your mates, they'll just help you eat it.

Eating outside the home is difficult, hanging around the chip shop or the local café is part of your social life and buying crisps and sweets in the corner shop is fun and self indulgent, and both foods you have to pay for yourself. At home it's all there for the taking, although if Mum is strict you'll ask her first before you raid the freezer and the cupboard, but if you're lucky she will buy the food you see advertised on telly.

The main meals, cooked by Mum, are the same as they ever were. The family usually sit down together for a meal in the evenings or Sunday lunch and that's often the only time they are all together. But Mum takes control of that and leaves the kids to make their own food the rest of the time. Cooking is not a hobby for the young, but it is part of their private face.

Despite the appeal of hobbies and other edifying activities, on the whole when asked what they did in their spare time, the kids' most popular pastime was still watching television and going out with friends, although an unpopular but major activity was also homework. When time wasn't taken up with these activities, it was mostly spent 'messing about':

'The bus shelter at the top of the road, everybody just meets there, every night, gangs, we just stand there.'

'Just have fun, enjoy yourself, don't care about anybody else – torment people.'

'Have friends round after school, Guides, youth clubs, just walking around, go round to friends' homes.'

'Walking around, looking for something to do.'

'Play the juke box, table tennis, listen to music, sit down and talk to your friends, move around, we talk about boys, school, fashions.'

'You just get fed up at home.'

8 The extreme face

The match

'Who the fucking hell are you?'

'What a bunch of wankers.'

'Tottenham Yids!'

'Right, clock in, do your job, go and get them, smash their heads in.'

'Sieg Heil! Sieg Heil! Sieg Heil!'

'It's like a chain reaction, mass hysteria. When everybody starts singing you can't resist it, even if you don't mean a word of it. No matter how gruesome the words are. It's just such a laugh. They start stamping their feet.'

'You can get your kidneys crushed. Remember when we went to Arsenal–Southampton, we were at the front and a goal was scored, and everyone surged forward doing "Knees up Mother Brown", and I got a bottle that hit me. Something hit me hard on the head. I looked round and no one was there.'

'You hear rumours that another team is going to bring up a whole lot of their hard nuts.'

'If the players get rough with each other the supporters take it out on each other, like say a Chelsea player had a disagreement with an Arsenal player, they saw him throw a couple of punches, some of the supporters start sharpening coins on the stone and they start throwing them into the opposing crowd.'

'They're really proud of it 'cause they've taken on another Shed. They think they've done something to help the honour of their football team. They use that as an excuse, most of them, to start trouble. Well, the leaders do anyway. The leaders are usually the more intelligent of the bunch but with the vicious streak in them. They can get the rest to do what they want. The trouble with them is, they can make themselves so good, whatever they talk about, however wrong it is, they can make it sound right. "It will give our team the name that we're really hardened, so we'll get respect." '

'Punks don't like Skinheads and they always fight. They're not going to know they are all Chelsea people – you just jump in and find out afterwards.'

'They start spitting or pissing on each other. The point will come when someone will say, "Come on, you reckon you are hard." When they start hurling really vicious abuse at each other, then you know something is going to happen. Then you just edge your way to the exits; if it comes your way, you just get out of it.'

'Some of them deliberately bring long pieces of wood, which have six-inch nails right the way through them, so they're sticking out of it, each side. Nowadays there's no limit. They won't say, "We'll beat him up but we'd better not cut him." Nowadays it's just anything really. Could be sort of hitting a bar on to his head and you just see his brains everywhere. Some of these hardnuts, they think it's a *real* laugh.'

'They'll start prodding you – "Come on then, what are you going to do about it?" – trying to provoke you. If that happens, you just walk away honestly.'

'You can't say, "Oh, I'd love to take you without that thing, that's fair enough isn't it?" He doesn't care. He'll just say "No" and just put it in your face.'

'It would be really stupid, you wouldn't fight just him. He'd have all his friends there and if he was losing, they'd all stick the boot in as well. They go round in bunches.'

'Today, it's hardness and toughness. It's different. You have to be really vicious to get a good name. You've got to be able to take punishment.'

'Outside the ground I was picked on. I just got pushed on the ground for some reason. I didn't know what I'd done.'

'They love to talk about how many times they've fought and then bend it a little bit. Like if they *did* chuck a bottle at somebody, they say, "Oh, I smashed a bottle first and then I rammed it into his head." They say, "Oh, the blood went all over my best suit," – you know, trying to be casual – "and I *just* bought it that day!" They take a pride in talking that way.'

'I don't go for the fighting when I go to football matches. I just go to watch the game and have a good sing song. I suppose I do chant at the other team, but if there's a fight I would probably run.'

'I've grown up with violence. I don't accept it but there's nothing I can do about it. I can't stop it. I know it sounds silly. I don't enjoy talking about it.'

Mike and Alistair are fifteen and they are talking about football violence. The boys insist they are not part of the violence. I am struck by their resentment as I urge them to describe how a fight actually starts. They are uneasy, unwilling to picture it. I expected them to be excited in spite of themselves. Instead they are edging away. As we sit talking in the car Alistair says 'There's one now, better keep quiet,' and he burrows down into his seat. A big bloke, with a shaven head, black leather jacket, short white cords and big black boots swaggers past, without giving them a second glance. They are scared.

I relent – we start talking about the cheeky songs instead. This is more like it. Yelling out, every voice in the crowd, deafening. An opposition player trips up Liam Brady, the honour of the Shed is at stake. The swearing trebles, abuse washes over the other side. Last time they baited the opposition goal keeper so much that he let a goal through. This is where the laughs are, exploding with aggression, egged on by the crowd, with all the righteousness of a knight defending the cause. But facing the wrong end of a piece of wood eighteen inches long, with nails sticking out on both sides, is not fun. Something has gone wrong.

Let's analyse what happens.

There is a home game on Saturday. By Tuesday, Mike and Alistair have arranged to go together. They wander round school seeing if they can persuade their mates to go. The alternative is parading round town, which they can do any Saturday, or watching telly. Three of them decide to go but Kevin backs out at the last minute because his mum won't let him. The other two are looking forward to it; there are old scores to settle with the away team and they expect to have fun. Mike dresses up in his boots and his leathers and winds on his team scarf. From this moment he takes on the identity of a supporter, and already he is freed from some of the usual constraints. He and his mate skip the bus fare and make for the ground laughing and cracking jokes loudly as they go. Mike's older brother slips them a can of lager each. They pass themselves off as fourteen, so they can get cheap tickets and choose a place up on the terraces at the end of the pitch. This is a defensive move. From past experience they know that the crowd in the centre stampedes on to the pitch when there's a goal, and they don't want to get crushed.

Already they are kidding themselves that they aren't part of the crowd, even though the reason they've come is to share the excitement and be lifted out of themselves. (They could have watched the match on telly after all.) The crowd builds, the excitement builds, people have been drinking. Mike and Alistair eye a group of Skinheads, taking up a position a few rows back; there are seven of them and they look hard. Mike takes a wary note of the escape routes, but doesn't change seats. Knowing the Skins are there heightens the risk and also the excitement. The game starts. Every manoeuvre on the field provokes a mammoth reaction in the crowd. Mike is singing his head off, Alistair is stamping and bawling at the stands opposite. The crowd is totally partisan, individual responsibility disappears. The noise is deafening. There's nothing they wouldn't do to those wankers on the other side. Where else could they experience such intensity?

During half-time, the Skins behind are throwing out insults at random. They have come to make trouble. They are now bored with singing and shouting and are looking for a fight.

Mike and Alistair ignore them. In the second half Mike feels a drop on his head and looks round to see them pissing on the people in front. Mike is angry, but wants to stay out of trouble. He's scared because he's younger than the Skins and besides he only has one mate with him. He throws himself into the match. The end of the game leaves him breathless, supercharged, looking for something to vent his aggression on. He and Alistair are ready to chase after the away team supporters and drive them off, if they can get at them. The supporters heave towards the gates, one of the Skins shoves into Mike and instantly swears at him for getting in the way. The gang turns on Mike, and Alistair insults them and laughs at them. To stand and take it is more than they can bear, so they shout back. Scared though they are, all the emotional residue of the game is ready to ignite. A man has to defend himself. The leader of the Skins is facing Mike now, challenging him to prove it. Up to this point no one has been hurt, this level of posturing is OK. But now, the leader has produced a weapon, he is prodding Mike with a nailed stick, as he tries to make it to the gate. This is definitely not OK, the shove might be accidental, but the weapon is deliberate. In a fight it could gash your face open. Mike knows that the Skinheads are looking for a fight, that they are expecting their leader to start it, and that the leader is an idiot and vicious. He has seen them before kneeing people in the balls and kicking them once they're down. If he fights, Mike knows he can't win, because there are seven of them with sticks and broken bottles. The unwritten rule says that you stop short of real injury, but the idiots are out for blood, something to brag about. Mike and Alistair are terrified, *they never thought it would happen to them*. When they'd been to matches before they had revelled in the emotional charge generated by the violence, but they'd never had to face the consequences themselves.

They have no option now but to get away if they can. Losing face is irrelevant when real injury threatens. They will only fight back if the Skinheads get them on the ground, and that will be a fight for survival. Ignoring the prods and shoves and insults, they push forward, get to the gate, where to their enormous relief they see a police cordon. The fight is averted, the Skins go off to provoke someone else away from the uniforms. There are scuffles and insults and people all round. Parts of the crowd are out of control, the away supporters are smashing the windows of a parked Cortina. Mike and Alistair have no heart for it. It's OK for the crowd to smash up a car, but they have been too close to the real thing. They slip away home. The boys are faced with a paradox. They go to the game for its intense excitement. Without the aggression the game would be commonplace. Every time they deny being involved in violence, they ignore the fact that violence heightens the risk, that risk heightens the thrill, and thrill is what they came for in the first place.

The more times they survive without a scratch, the more they kid themselves that nothing will happen to them and the less responsible they feel. When events run out of control, they are scared and look to adults to re-establish order.

Taking responsibility

The football match highlights major dilemmas facing teenagers as they struggle to evolve a code of behaviour. Their task is to experience as wide a range of sensation as they can, and to learn at first hand what will hurt them and what won't. At the same time, they have to learn not to hurt other people; in other words to act morally as well as selfishly. They are not mini-adults, they don't have the perspective to make *wise* decisions, they are influenced by the obvious consequences of their actions.

Beverly at thirteen has been smoking for a long time. 'I'm bothered in a way, but I've smoked that much and it hasn't affected me yet. You got to get all tar round your heart I mean ...' She rejects the idea of hard drugs because all her friends say she could get hooked, but she has been sniffing glue, because glue is harmless isn't it? It's on sale in W. H. Smith and she's used it at school. 'I smelt this glue, it smelt like fresh bread, just come out of the oven.'

Lawrence Kohlberg at Harvard has suggested that all of us learn morality by going through a number of different stages. In the first stage we make moral decisions according to whether or not we shall get hurt, in the second stage according to what we have been told to do, and in the third according to what we think will please other people. The fourth, fifth and sixth stages are concerned with obeying the law of the land and working out your own independent value system. The idea is that once you have reached a new stage, you add the new way of thinking on to the old ones and by the end you are acting from a sense of personal responsibility.

The teenagers I talked to were trying to solve new moral problems every day and they were using the three initial approaches, phrased as: 'Will I get caught?' 'My Mum says ...' 'They won't like it if I ...' In most cases they were reacting to external constraints rather than an inner voice. Mike and Alistair walked away from the fight at the match because they were going to get hurt, not because they believed that fighting itself was wrong. Michelle feels guilty about sleeping with her boy-friend, not because she believes that sex is wrong, but because her mother wouldn't like it.

Authorities are fair game.

Wherever adults lay down formal rules ('My mum told me not to stay out later than 10 p.m.' 'You're not allowed to drink until you're sixteen') teenagers feel at liberty to challenge them. The deciding factor is whether or not they can get away with it. If the punishment is severe enough, they won't bother to try. Michelle at sixteen knows that she's not supposed to nick things. She draws the line at nicking make-up from Boots, because she knows she'll be in 'real trouble' if they catch her, but she nicks paint brushes from her art class at school because the worst that could happen is being called up in front of the Headmistress. 'You nick pencils and paint brushes from art class at school; if you get into trouble, you don't mind so much. Stealing from shops you know you are going to get into real trouble if you're caught.' Simon at twelve gets a thrill from listening to the police band on the radio. He knows it's illegal, but even if they catch him, he'll only get a warning: 'Well it's not you that's going to get fined, it's your mum and dad!'

Daring the limits set by authority is the way to prove you're not a child. Taking risks is exciting. Simon, Beverly and Michelle don't feel personal responsibility for doing something wrong, because it's not wrong unless they're caught. It's up to the legislators to enforce the law, and to punish them if they can catch them.

They build up moral responsibility through their friends, not

125

by breaching the rules of the establishment. If a friend is in trouble they are obliged to help. Everyone belongs to a group, and the group has a right to demand loyalty. If the Skinhead gang had attacked Mike on the terraces, then Alistair was duty bound to stay and fight even though he knew he would get hurt. If Beverly is upset because her parents have been arguing, then Sarah is duty bound to let her copy the next day's homework even though her teacher says she mustn't. If Andy sees Kevin skipping school at break-time, he is honour bound not to 'grass' on him.

Now if parents suddenly become accomplices instead of law givers, they become eligible for the same privileges. If Mum is always short of money then Stephen must go out and earn his own money, rather than pester her for more. If Michelle's mum tells her it's OK to smoke pot, but not to do it in the house because the police might nick her, then Michelle is honour bound to smoke outside.

Taking responsibility is not easy, and teenagers are schizophrenic about it. Andy at fifteen may drink half a bottle of whisky at a party, but if his little brother is there too, he will watch to see that the kid doesn't drink more than is good for him.

So two different moralities grow up, one for equals and one for authority. The third area is even more difficult – responsibility to *yourself*. Michelle is experimenting with smoking, drinking, drugs and sex; she wants to sample every sensation going. She's not hurting anyone else, but all the same, Mum and the law are telling her she's not supposed to. Her friends are all doing it – how is she supposed to decide?

'A friend of mine, she got really high once and she walked out of a second-floor window; she just walked out.'

'I think what put me off, even if I wanted to smoke, was my grandmother died, and my mother stopped smoking.'

It is a balancing act, between Mum hammering home the lurid consequences and friends demonstrating that you can do them all and survive. When Michelle has seen one of her friends get pregnant, another walk off a second-storey balcony under the influence of drugs, and her grandmother die of lung cancer, she can decide for herself how far she wants to go. Until then, it's up to Mum to set the rules and apply the sanctions.

The teenage code

Unlike the Ten Commandments, which God conveniently summarized for Moses on a tablet of stone, the teenage code is picked up piecemeal. It is surprisingly consistent. I am shocked to find how extreme it is; right is right and wrong is wrong and should be punished. As Alistair said, you need someone who knows what they're doing and not biased in favour of the kids:

'You've got a Juvenile court and most of the magistrates there are just part time. They've got their yachts waiting for them. They've got no idea of the real world. So much money that everything's kept away from them. They don't realize what's going on so they're not the people who should be in the hot seat. You need someone who knows about the real problems. A social worker would be the ideal person, but she would probably have a bias towards the youth.'

Murderers should be hanged, life sentences should be for life. Prisoners in Borstals should be put on bread and water, and they certainly shouldn't be given chicken on Christmas Day. At least, in Harry's opinion:

'They say it's three to a cell and stuff like that, but they still get good dinners don't they? Christmas they get chicken and all. They're there to be punished, I wouldn't give them luxuries. People stealing cars are just put away for six months and then they come out and do it again.'

Justice is black and white, but there must be shades of grey somewhere. Let's have a close look at what is OK and what is not and see how the code emerges.

It is always OK to fight to defend yourself. If you had nothing to do with provoking an attack, then in theory anything goes. Harry, sixteen, would pretend to give in and secretly get out his knife (he avoids describing how he would use it). Kevin at fourteen swears he would shoot someone who broke into his house, and if it's them or you then it's OK to kill them:

'If someone came in, I'd shoot their arms off and make them sorry. You can use combs to stab someone, a flick knife. I'd use it if someone came for me. If someone attacks you, you go for the stomach, really go mad, scar his face maybe. If he's got a weapon, you'd try to knock it out of his arm – no I wouldn't, I'd run!'

Better for an adult to take responsibility though.

'If my dad was soft, I'd be embarrassed. My dad went to Belgium on a trip, and there was this man laying in the road, and me dad went to pick him up, and this man hit him in the face, and me dad got really annoyed. But he said, "Come on," and he helped him up, and he hit me dad in the face again. So my dad just hit him. He hit him that hard he broke his jaw.'

Beverly's father had every justification for knocking out his assailant, because he'd tried to help first.

Boys understand that you have to prove your manhood. It's OK to break the law. You can drink alcohol, get into an X-film under age and score with your girl if she'll let you. Girls too, accept that it's OK to smoke and drink for the sake of your social image: 'I enjoy it. I started when I was going out with this guy who smoked, so I began. You go to parties and everyone else is and you're not, so I started too.' It's OK to gamble at school, swear at the away team and fight to defend your honour as long as you don't do any serious damage. It's OK to muck about in class, set fire to a toilet roll in the loo, and brag about your exploits. No one will challenge you if you put on a hard front about how much you like the violence on TV. Harry sums it up, and he doesn't consider himself one of the real nutters: 'You get documentaries on television about wars, and thirteen- and fourteen-year-old kids come into school and laugh about it. I think they put on a front with their mates. But about ten per cent will really laugh at it. Real nutters.'

Fantasy violence is not only OK, it is highly desirable. As long as they're safely on the screen, boys drool over car crashes, car chases, fist fights, swearing, shoot-outs and a mangled blonde. Says Harry: 'I got into my first AA film when I was eleven. I had to wear jeans and Doc Martins and a coat and everything to look older. It was only AA because of the language – a lot of swearing, four-letter words. Also a bloke was chopped up by machetes, that might have been the other reason.' But Andy is adamant about its fantasy status: 'I like violence, like at our age we like watching fights on the telly; fights I don't think are that bad. You don't go out and kick someone in after you've seen "The Sweeney".'

The girls exult over horror movies and gleefully savour the stake being plunged into Dracula's heart.

But if someone commits a real crime, the kids show no mercy. They insist on matching the punishment to the crime. Murderers deserve to be hanged – 'It's cheaper too!'. Criminal teenagers should be given the 'short, sharp shock' treatment, otherwise they would just go out and do it again.

Michelle at sixteen: 'I think hanging should come back, and then they wouldn't kill people. They should have heavier sentences for rapists as well.'

Harry at sixteen: 'Those detention centres they've brought out are a good idea. They're like Colditz. That would stop us shoplifting. It would scare you, so you wouldn't do it again.'

If there's a law, then it's OK to enforce it. It's OK to have a bouncer in a record shop if the Skins are planning to fight the Punks inside and it's OK to have a police force to protect you.

Andy is tough but not stupid: 'If something happens, then you really want the police to be there; if you get stabbed or something. People say they hate the police just to impress, like they say the police are pigs. If you're at a football match, everybody joins in shouting "Nick, nick, nick, nick ..."'

But it was the police cordon which saved Mike and Alistair from being beaten up at the match. The police are a safety net for when things get out of hand, so is Mum and so is the law. It is essential for Mum to forbid you to smoke, and it's OK to have a law making pot illegal. You may break the boundaries, but at least you know they're there.

Crimes have to be punished, but some things don't count as crimes. Nicking from an institution is so impersonal that nobody gets hurt, and there is everything to gain. It's OK to nick car parts, if you happen to work for Godfrey Davis, and it's OK to nick enough spares out of the Army to build your own rifle (although you have to watch that you don't blow yourself up). Nicking for a dare is part of proving yourself and it has the added advantage that you don't have to pay for the sweets, pencils, eye shadow etc. out of your limited pocket money. Taping off the radio is another illegal activity which does no obvious harm to anyone and everyone does it without a qualm.

So far, in the Code, no teenager has willingly inflicted injury on anyone else. The kids are afraid of hurting anyone and of being hurt themselves. But if you *are* unavoidably hurt or unhappy then it is OK to seek refuge in drink, smoking or drugs, even suicide. Take Beverly: 'I wouldn't commit suicide – well I would if my sister died or got run over; I've only got my grandad, like. There's nothing – I couldn't care.'

'If you're lonely, or you don't have a family, or your family ill-treats you then you can take pot to forget it – that's what Pop Stars do. They've not got any family life. They're out at discotheques doing shows and they go and take drugs for the sake of it,' Simon explains. But even so, things have to be pretty bad. Take Beverly's friend: 'She took it because her mother died when she was only young, her dad used to beat her up and she ran away from home and he brought her back and beat her up and tried things on with her. She took drugs to make her feel happy.' 'I think that the people who turn to it have either lost someone in the family or have knocked someone down and killed them.'

Smoking is less extreme. It's OK to smoke if the rest of the gang is smoking. For boys it's a normal manhood dare, but girls need to justify it. It's OK if you need something to keep you occupied, when you're nervous talking to boys, it's something to do with your hands. It's one way of coping with stress, and besides your dad smokes. Anyway it's up to you if you decide to chuck your health away.

So if you ask Simon, Beverly, Andy, Michelle and Harry, you'll find it's OK to defend yourself and dare the rules, as long as there are strict punishments for going too far. It's OK to pack in all the thrills you can as long as you don't have to face anybody getting hurt (and that includes yourself).

And what's not OK is precisely the reverse. What are the limits? Murder is the most terrifying crime of all, death is irreversible, the Yorkshire Ripper inspires horror. It's not OK to shoot someone in real life or blow people up, or kill someone who's done nothing to you, or show such realistic murder in a film that it looks as though it really happened. Such as in *The Warriors*: 'I don't think that should ever have been released. It wasn't just fighting and punching – it was all different killings, flick knives, lead piping. I can't believe nothing like that would happen. It's violence you'd see today, but it's a bit far fetched. I don't think gangs would kill each other. Not like that, not lead piping.'

Aggression is OK, but violence is not. Pointless unprovoked violence is frightening. It's not OK to push old biddies around, it's not OK for the police to beat you up with truncheons, and it's not OK to smack someone in the mouth, just for staring. It's not OK to use weapons when you're angry because you could really do damage. Mike and Alistair couldn't fight against the Skinheads' nailed sticks at the match. Gang violence is tricky, they hate it but the rules are clear. You know Skinheads are going to be violent and you have to avoid them as you would a live volcano. It's only the 'nutters' and 'idiots' who start fights and revel in physical injury. But it's not OK to be soft, either; you can't just walk away from people giving you dirty looks and calling you names. Manhood lies half-way between dares and violence.

Somehow you have to avoid going beyond the point of no return. (It's OK to gamble at school but not with pound notes.) It's not OK to get caught up in a mass riot, lose your temper all the time, or to drink alcohol just so you feel ready to fight anybody or go further with boys. 'When you drink, you could drink too much, you could do anything. You could steal something or you could get yourself pregnant or anything. When you smoke, you can keep yourself.' You can experiment with pot and glue sniffing, but you mustn't get hooked on the hard stuff. Michelle knows her own limits. 'I don't want to get into heroin, I don't want to get into acid. But something that I can't get addicted to I can get into, like drinking.

I won't get addicted to that. If I'm bored I go round and have a smoke with someone.'

It's important to retain the right image in the eyes of your friends. It's not OK to look like a slag, nor must you look stupid or out of your head. Michelle reckons that one advantage to pot is that you look better stoned than drunk.

So far the taboos have all been concerned with the consequences to Number One. When it comes to friends, the responsibility is mutual. You don't nick from your friend's school bag and you don't nick anything out of his mum's house. If you know he's put a lot of effort into building up his racer, you don't wreck it for him. If you said you would go to the disco with your best friend, then you go. Loyalty to your friends takes precedence over loyalty to authority. You don't grass on your mate, and he has the right to 'kick your head in' if you do. Nor do you betray a confidence; Beverly never forgave Julie for spreading it round the school that she'd had a row with her dad.

But there are still injustices amongst your peers. Bullies frightened Simon and Sarah when they went up to the comprehensive school, gangs from neighbouring schools stage ritual fights, unwanted Hell's Angels move in and spoil your disco. Joanne was angry and ashamed: 'A lot of the Hell's Angels come from their dance and nobody dare move when they come. I feel ashamed. They ruin it for us and themselves. They gave us the disco and now they have ruined it. They wreck everything and you feel like going up to them and saying "You horrible mean things" and smashing one. You just can't.'

It is not OK to bully kids smaller than yourself or break up a party, but there is no way for adults to enforce justice here. Teenagers have to fight it out for themselves. When the Skinheads were pissing on Mike and Alistair at the match, no adult could have settled things for them. You have to trust your friends and they must not break your trust. It's OK to brag, but not to lie.

Also you are honour bound to protect kids younger than you. You can swear like a trooper and smoke like a chimney yourself, but it's not OK to give cigarettes to eight and nine-year-olds or teach them swear words. It's not OK to lead your younger brothers and sisters astray. At thirteen, Beverly is not going to let anything happen to her little sister: 'It's wrong to give little kids a cigarette. He wanted to give her a cigar and I had to break it up and chuck it outside. I wouldn't let her touch it.'

Grey areas

The system depends on adults setting the rules and carrying them out to the letter. Teenagers can cope with only a limited degree of subtlety. The worst crime, next to murder, is adult hypocrisy; it undermines the whole system. It is not OK for the police to shake you down and steal your boots, or pick you up for loitering if you weren't doing anything.

It is terrifying when a crowd of drunken men threaten you with broken bottles.

Michelle: 'I was in Soho, I think there was only about six of us. There was a group of men lined up outside a pub. They were really drunk. As we walked past, one of them came up to a friend of mine with a glass in his hand, smashed it on the wall and threatened him to not walk past him again. So what do you do? There were grown-up men standing in front of you. I was really scared. Nothing like that has ever happened to me before.'

It is not OK for teachers to tell you not to smoke and then do so themselves. It is not OK for teachers to forbid you to gamble at school, take bets on the Rugby International, and *then* not pay up when they lose. It goes even deeper. It is not OK for teachers to tell you to work hard at school and then not bother to teach you properly; and it is not OK for parents to tell you to control your behaviour and then to argue with one another themselves. It is not OK to let Paul McCartney off a jail sentence, just because he's famous.

I was surprised how clearly the kids understood the dangers and avoided the extremes. By common consent, it was the idiots and thicks who went over the line. In Andy's words: 'The thicks go round in Dr Martins and they try to be hard. Then you've got the clever lot, who are really just sensible, but they could beat up the idiots. So when the idots start doing over some soft kid that we know, we just go out and sort out all the thicks. Generally in our school it's just the morons who smoke. The clever kids have either tried one before and just think it's horrible, although you do get a few clever ones that smoke. You usually find that if you get all the tough nuts and the kids who smoke and sniff glue, they're nearly always the lower bands, they don't do their work.'

'The kids that are the real mad ones – it's not always because they've got bad backgrounds, it's usually only the excuse.'

It is the grey areas which pose the problems.

On violence: When is it OK to run away and when do you have to stay and fight? What do you do if you've got a girl with you? Is it OK to run down your friends if you're trying to impress another gang? Do the Punks have a right to attack you if you're wearing your Mod tie? Stephen doesn't complain:

'I was out one lunch-time, carrying two take-away coffees, and I was wearing a Mod tie, and some Punks attacked me. I got smashed in the mouth – the coffee went all over me. It happened because of what you are. They've got something against each other.'

On nicking: Is it a dare or a crime to nick from mum's handbag, knowing nothing terrible is going to happen to you? Is it OK to nick a bike, when you don't know who owns it, but it's likely to be a boy like you?

The more personal the consequences and concrete the punishment, the easier it is to decide. If Beverly has to face the lady whose handbag she nicked in the loo, she won't nick it. If Andy gets beaten up for wearing his red tie, he'll think twice next time. If they can't *see* the results of their actions, then it may be up to adults to tell them. Thanks to anti-smoking propaganda three-quarters of today's teenagers disagree with smoking even though many have tried it. Most kids sample their first alcoholic drink at Sunday lunch because Mum and Dad give it to them. Nineteen out of twenty teenagers don't believe alcohol will harm them.

Teenagers have a lively desire to keep out of harm's way, they hate violence, and they love aggression, and they are experimenting with every new sensation which comes their way. They depend on authority to set the rules and enforce them without leniency. This is to keep them safe so that, in the meantime, they can work out their own moral code.

The teenage commandments

1 Thou shalt not murder or cause physical injury to anybody, unless you're a Skinhead, and then I know to keep well clear of you.
2 If thou commit a crime thou shalt be punished for it to the letter of the law, and not be given chicken on Christmas Day if you're in Borstal.
3 Thou shalt not start a fight unprovoked but if thou art, thou mayest fight back with everything you've got.
4 Adults shall lay down the law and stick to it themselves and not tell you to stop smoking, while puffing away on a fag.
5 Thou shalt stand by thy mates and neither grass on them nor nick from them, and listen to their problems when they are troubled.
6 Thou shalt cram in as many different sensations as thou canst come by.
7 Thou shalt never become addicted nor go beyond the point of no return; it is better to run away than to be crushed.
8 Thou mayest soften thy mental anguish by resorting to drugs and drink, but not just for the sake of it.
9 Thou shalt prove thy manhood and womanhood by daring the establishment and thou mayst nick sweets for kicks as long as you don't personally upset anybody.
10 Thou shalt not lead astray thy younger brother and sister, however depraved you may be yourself!

9 Swamped by ideas

What role does the media play in the life of a modern adolescent?

The 'media' isn't a word ever used by teenagers. They see television, radio, books, magazines, newspapers, advertising, cinema as forms of entertainment and they judge them on that basis alone.

Television

In a recent film Peter Sellers made a comment on a real life event: 'It's better than on television', and it was meant to be funny, but the adolescents we talked to often reacted the same way and couldn't see any humour in the remark.

After home and school, television has the most influence on modern kids. The appreciation of the role and effect of television is another of the vital keys to understanding the young. If we think about what they watch, maybe we begin to understand why they talk and act the way they do. Of all the people we interviewed three out of four of them watched television for an average of 3–4 hours every night. Younger girls tended to watch it the most. This fact gives a clue to one of the main uses of television – as a form of entertainment. Many girls watch it for six hours a night. They told me how they switched the TV on when they got home from school and then watched it until they went to bed at night. What else did they have to do? If they had any homework it would probably get done in front of the TV, likewise any hobbies or practical pursuits could be done in the presence of the 'box'. They didn't go out much; they were either too young or their parents too strict with them. It was basically a choice between going out or staying in and watching telly. Mary understood this well. She was fifteen and kept telling me how she suffered from two major afflictions – she was small, and so looked younger than she was, and she had strict parents who tended to be over protective. She was always moaning about what she wasn't allowed to do and felt life treated her very unfairly, especially compared to her older looking friends at school. They are sleeping with their boy-friends, but not Mary: 'I watch everything on television. I don't go out anywhere so I watch it all.' Beverly had to stay in on Fridays: 'I watch TV every Friday because there's nobody in. I'm not allowed out in case I'm involved in anything. You never know, a man could easily come up to you.'

The amount of television they watched tended to drop off with age. As the boys and girls grew older and developed interests outside their home, they watched less television, for they were beginning to experience life first hand, and the excitement of the TV screen began to wane. The most dramatic drop off in viewing was amongst girls of fifteen and sixteen, understandably, as they were too interested in boys and going to discos to bother with television. They were also at that stage of rejecting the family's dependence on telly, and moving away from family viewing. Girls like Michelle and Debbie wanted to be independent and make their own choices.

Apart from these older kids, we gained the very clear impression that television was a life support system to most of the rest of the kids and that they would be totally lost without it:

'The place would seem boring without it.'

'I love telly, I watch it every night, I don't know what I'd have done if I lived about thirty years ago, it must have been awful.'

Kids aren't the only ones who rely on television to fill their spare time. Mum and Dad and any other family members watch too. It really is a case of the family viewing together. Most families eat together in the evening – the main meal of the day – and then they watch telly. There is very little verbal communication between them, either about the television programmes or anything else. They seem to be letting the media, particularly television, carry out the conversations for them and they just observe passively. Anyway, television is a captivating medium in itself.

The young adolescent doesn't mind watching so much television because it is both entertaining and informing and is a way of learning – 'the window on the world'. Rejection of television, however, seems to be one of the signs of growing up and maturing. Mary moaned that her lack of physical maturity restricted her fun to the television. Michelle and Debbie, while barely a year older, got their fun first hand. They had boy-friends, went around in a gang, stayed out late at parties, drank in pubs – out doing all the things teenagers are seen to do. They had their favourite television programmes but generally rejected the 'box'. They hated the way the family sat round it and watched in silence. The two girls wanted the freedom to choose, to search out their own ideas and personal identity. They would rather go out or else go to their room to read, play records, listen to the radio, even watch their own television as long as they felt they were making a personal choice rather than being dictated to: 'I hate the way they all just sit there and watch it.'

So television seems to be most important to the adolescent who is still very much at home and has not begun to move away. For them, television both entertains and informs, but it is difficult to split apart these two functions as television teaches in such an entertaining manner, and what may seem like pure entertainment to adults, is a source of learning for kids. Add to this the range of programmes they watch. The television stations may separate programmes up into children's television, news programmes, family entertainment and adult programmes but the young today watch it all.

Comedy
On a purely entertainment level, what the young of all ages enjoy most is the comedy programmes: 'I watch every comedy programme there is.' They have a tremendous sense of humour and can turn nearly everything into a joke: 'If you've not got a sense of humour you're boring.' With their wise naïveté they see their favourite programmes as containing a brand of humour that is unique to them and their friends. They see it as having no appeal to parents – and usually it doesn't. 'Parents only like straight things. They don't like things like "Fawlty

Towers" because that's a bit warped.' Kenny Everett was probably the TV personality most popular with all ages and both boys and girls. His off-beat silly zaniness was something they could relate to and his air of naughtiness or mischief strengthened their identification with him. It was almost as if they could imagine him 'messing around' and being naughty at school, so he was an idol in the whole 'them and us' syndrome. There seemed little regional variation with favourite television programmes and thirteen-year-old Beverly from Warrington summed up the appeal of Kenny Everett in just the same way as an eleven-year-old in Bristol or a sixteen-year-old in London.

'My Mum hates him, says he's mad ... but he's great, really great, he's so stupid he makes you laugh, tells jokes in a funny voice and pretends when he's on it's not him, I love him.'

'My Mum hates him,' and that must be one of the main reasons for his popularity. Benny Hill was also very popular but he seemed to be most popular with the boys. This was a completely different type of humour to Kenny Everett, the off-beat hero. Benny Hill probably corresponded more closely with the playground humour of the boys. He was more earthy and used fairly crude sexual connotations that are understood by any school boy or girl. Kenny Everett, however, particularly with Hot Gossip, was more sophisticated sexually. Kevin, a typical fourteen-year-old, commented on the difference between the two although he was keen on both.

'Benny Hill's different to Kenny Everett. Kenny Everett is disgusting but Benny Hill runs them into humour and he makes them funny.'

This suggests that kids are not always as sophisticated as they seem. 'Carry on' films were also very popular with everyone and were much in the same vein as Benny Hill – fun, frolicks and innuendo. As Frances describes: 'Carry on Camping was good. She goes swimming, and an animal comes out and nicks all her clothes, and she's left there with this man ...' And a group of twelve-year-old girls dissolve into laughter and hysterics and go on to describe endless 'Carry on' scenes where the girl is caught undressed. It all fits in with their self-conscious attitudes to their own body and their fear of embarrassment.

Age did play some part in the popularity of comedy programmes. 'Tiswas', 'Swapshop' and 'Laurel and Hardy' were
loved by the under-thirteens. They related to the slapstick
humour, it was an extension of 'messing about' and the idea of
throwing a custard pie at an adult, as in 'Tiswas', linked into
their more down to earth fantasies:

' "Tiswas" is great, it's stupid, and they throw all that gungey
stuff at everybody, it's nutty, but it's great.'

'It's a young version of "Monty Python".'

The older and more sophisticated teenagers we talked to
preferred the minority and more esoteric comedies such as
'Soap', 'Fawlty Towers', 'Reginald Perrin', 'Monty Python',
'Mash' and 'The Goodies'. These programmes were picked
both for their fun and silliness, as well as their satire and the
fact that they are all original. Also the teenagers' enjoyment
was heightened by parental disapproval and dislike. It helped
create a feeling of separateness. The element of satire is important. All these favourites in some way parody adult society
in the form of the family, television, hotels, business etc. – a
highly relevant attitude for the young teenager who is in this
invidious position of being neither child nor adult, in a sort of
limbo land. Nevertheless, it is a time for observing and storing
up ideas about life, whilst at the same time the kids don't really
know what to make of what they are seeing. How could they?
They have no personal experience of it.

That is until they watch a programme like 'Soap' or 'Fawlty
Towers'. Suddenly they recognize it all; they see the stupidity
and hypocrisy in adult behaviour and they can join in and
laugh. Probably the reason many adults/parents do not appreciate these programmes is that they are too close to the satire
to see it, or want to see it, wihout feeling threatened.

'My mum doesn't like anything like "Monty Python" or
"Fawlty Towers", she just doesn't find them funny.'

'We have competitions in school to try and guess what will
happen next week in "Soap".'

'I love "Soap", it's brilliant. Burt's the best one, when he's
drunk, did you see it and he was trying to stand on the table
and his legs are wobbling ... I didn't like it so much when he

140

was in the spaceship but then Billy is good, where he's in love with his teacher.'

It's not surprising Carol didn't like the space ship episodes because they are physically outside the environment of the satire in home and school.

They watched all the comedy programmes and although the sitcom series were liked they did not get the acclaim of the others. They are not so continually and consistently funny. Overall, comedy programmes are really the only pure entertainment programmes for the young, as all the others have a high degree of educational value.

Kitchen sink

Education is meant in the broadest sense, yet adolescents spend a lot of energy learning about life, in a limbo land somewhere between home, school and the outside world. Their lives are really very limited. They know little about what goes on outside their immediate environment, yet they are eager and keen to learn and discover. School has given them the taste for knowledge but they want to see if it is right. Are their parents and friends right? Are they themselves in line with other young people? After all, how do they know they're not freaks? Part of the appeal of a programme like 'Top of the Pops' is looking at the audience and trying to assess whether or not they look like you and your friends : 'It helps you to keep in touch, to see what everyone's like, to see what they're all meaning.'

'Dallas' and 'Coronation Street' provide the young with ideas about family life as lived by others. Both these programmes are very popular, particularly with the girls. Sarah lives in the south and is a great fan of 'Coronation Street' : 'It tells you about family life in their road, different people, what they do and what could happen – it's good, I enjoy it.' She can relate easily to the family situations and she enjoys finding out how they cope with their everyday lives; it's quite reassuring to recognize similarities.

'Dallas' is rather more exciting because it deals with family life in Texas but it keeps to the stereotype characters they are familiar with in American life. It's not really that far from

'Coronation Street' in emotions but it extends the teenagers' experience by dealing with America and they are convinced that the characters in 'Dallas' are typical of all Americans. Debbie feels that 'Coronation Street' is very mediocre and small time in comparison:

'It's much more exciting, they go more places, they're out in the country, there are horses and they go riding. It's about a family, whereas "Coronation Street" is only about old women going to the shops and buying half a pound of this, that and the other.'

Drama

Everyone wants to be scared, thrilled and frightened, but in the safety of their own homes, and this was why detectives, horror or thriller films were so popular. Whether it's James Bond, 'The Sweeney', or 'Streets of San Francisco', they have gripping, involving storylines that captivate young and old alike.

Gerald is a fourteen-year-old living in Newcastle. He loves detectives, particularly the more violent type. He is no different to any average fourteen-year-old boy – he's boisterous and lively and lives in a nice suburban home in a happy family environment. He's no 'social problem' or delinquent. But when he told me about the appeal of violence I was horrified until I talked and listened to others like him. It is the action and thrill in the violent scenes that they like so much; they are as horrified as anyone else at the thought of *real* violence. But on the cinema or TV screen it's not real, it's removed. When it did seem real, they recoiled.

'*The Warriors*, I don't think that should ever have been released. My mate in the second year got in and he said it was horrible to think that something like that was happening. It isn't just fighting and punching, it was all different killings. Flick knives, lead piping. I can't believe that would happen.'

They experience the excitement without the pain, and by comparison, the intervening scenes often seem very dull.

Gerald was describing *French Connection 2*: 'It was good, it was realistic, they had him on drugs and the criminals got him, he was set up to try and catch some drug dealers ... it got quite boring in the middle though, when he was just walking the streets trying to find clues, but it brightens up when there was a fight at the end down by the docks and there was a gun battle with machine guns firing all over the place ... and Gene Hackman chased the guy in charge and shot him in the head and that was the end of the film. I don't really like it so much when they get killed, it's just that it's exciting.'

Gerald's attitude is not unusual, they all seem most interested in the excitement and the rush of adrenalin which goes with the fear: 'Carrie was good. It wasn't a pleasure, but I was scared for a week and a half afterwards.'

Maybe adolescents are too young to appreciate drama. Plays were noticeable by their absence in their list of favourites. Dramatic scenes frequently rely on subtle factors such as inflections, looks, voice tones, and the young are not ready for this. They need all their messages to be obvious and to involve excitement or humour.

They are also looking for realism. It makes the excitement more powerful. Which is why 'The Sweeney' or 'Shoestring' scores over 'Streets of San Francisco': 'Our films are more realistic, more life-like. In America they're always running down the streets firing at each other but Eddie Shoestring is more down to earth.'

British TV films and series are considered to be far superior to the American – partly because they use a more realistic environment that the kids can relate to but also because the stories are usually more interesting and less predictable.

'There's too much Yankee trash on TV; that's all they seem to have, detectives who always win and find what they're looking for. I prefer the British ones.'

'American stuff is all the same rubbish, detectives are all the same, just different names.'

'American things are usually corny and not realistic, the English do it much better.'

'Starsky and Hutch' was often quoted as the example of an American TV series. Although exciting, the thrill is diluted because they are always running and seem too good to be true.

It wasn't only in thrillers that the kids criticized the Americans. They perceive a great gulf between our styles of humour, and see the British as infinitely superior.

'They laugh at anything there. In England you've got to have an intelligent joke to get a laugh.'

'They just wouldn't understand "Monty Python" or "Fawlty Towers".'

Sex

There was no comment or sign from the children that their parents had ever complained, or criticized, or censored programmes because of violence. It was not the case though with sex. Not only were the boys and girls highly self-conscious about sex, but so it seemed were their parents.

'The Kenny Everett Show' and Hot Gossip was causing all the fuss when we were talking to these kids and is a good example of the way the two generations react. The younger boys and girls told me with glee in their eyes how their parents disapproved of and hated Hot Gossip.

'My dad says they're like prostitutes.'

'My mum says they're not very nice.'

But the kids themselves are confused about the values involved. They realize the programme is 'rude' and naughty because of the way their parents react and because the dancers wear revealing clothes but at the same time they look good, are great dancers and they themselves would do anything to dance like that. The way fourteen-year-old Beverly reacted to Hot Gossip shows this confusion.

'They're a bit rude, you can see their bust and everything. I love their costumes, they're all shiny and silk ... but they're the world's greatest dancers ... I'd love to be able to dance like that although I could never wear those clothes.'

Parents approve of Benny Hill or Dick Emery yet are filled with distaste for Hot Gossip. Most of the younger boys and girls didn't really understand why.

'My dad says they're like prostitutes, but I had to ask my mum what prostitutes meant.'

'They're all touching their bodies, and some of their movements are a bit silly, you'd never dance like that in a disco!'

Andrew however summed up one male point of view. 'Disgusting but cor!'

Apart from these comedy shows there were really very few

144

comments from the young themselves about sex on television. Maybe they were too embarrassed to raise the subject, but it might also be that they don't really understand it. They know about playground jokes, but for most of them sexual experiences are in the future and they do not always understand the subtleties in an adult programme. They certainly watch many adult films, as thirteen-year-old Stephen tells me:

'There was one on the other night with David Essex, he was a bit of a stud, he had more women in bed than he had hairs on his chest – but you didn't actually see anything rough.'

Kevin was fifteen yet he had never been restricted by his parents about what he watched:

'They don't stop me watching any programmes. Anyway, if I want to watch them I can as I've got a TV in my bedroom.'

A quarter of the children interviewed had their own TV sets so Kevin's remark was not unusual. When there was sex on television, as with Hot Gossip on the film that Ian described, they did not always find it comfortable viewing:

'My mum gets embarrassed and goes out to make the tea. She looks at you to see if you're watching and you pretend you're not watching ... it's awful, you don't know what to do.'

It's not surprising really that the young are so mixed up about sex.

Specially aimed
Some things though were actually worse in the eyes of parents than sex – 'Grange Hill'. Of course not all parents would see the programme because it is on children's television, but many who did disapproved. Yet the kids loved it. It was one of their favourite programmes. It seemed to be the first TV series that actually related to school children on their own level, and that was appreciated. One thing the kids understand is school. 'Grange Hill' is a comprehensive school as it really is, in the raw. Those who were at comprehensives liked it because it reflected their lives and those who didn't could still recognize it and wish they could get up to all those things. It was an adolescent's real life kitchen sink drama and they loved it.

'"Grange Hill" is all about school kids like us, the things that go on at their schools.'

'Real life in a comprehensive. Basically, it's what goes on ... it's supposed to be very controversial because adults don't think that's what goes on. They even had a programme called "The Grange Hill Debate".'

While the kids enjoy the series because it is aimed at them personally, many parents seem to find it threatening: 'I think it's brilliant, but I'm not allowed to watch it.' Those parents who accept 'Grange Hill' are considered a bit naïve by their children: 'Mum and Dad quite like it, but they don't think it really happens, they don't believe it – but it is what goes on.' It's ironic that the one programme that seems true to life for the young, and that they feel closest to, is criticized so much by adults.

Mixed views were expressed towards children's television. Not all the teenagers watched it. Much depended on whether they stayed at school late; how long it took to get home; whether or not they did their homework straight after school etc. 'Grange Hill' was certainly one programme they would actually change plans in order to watch. 'Blue Peter' was quite popular because it had a range of items, but much was dependent upon the appeal of the presenters. The trouble with children's television was that it was difficult to appeal equally to ages varying from eleven to sixteen, but Andy who was fourteen and right in the middle of the age group, felt the problem was: 'We watch all the adult programmes but there's hardly anything for teenagers – so we just watch what's on.'

On the whole, however, the BBC had a much better image with the young because they were felt to be actually making the odd attempt to cater for them.

It is with space adventure though, that television (and cinema) excell as a medium for these kids. Books and magazines are fine but you need to see the 'real thing' on the screen. The TV screen is good for the action and special effects and is thought to get much closer to their fantasy of space and space travel than words ever can. John and Stewart are two fans who agree on the supremacy of television and its ability as a medium to make fantasy come to life:

'The special effects are so much better than in magazines. With those you're only reading, but on TV you can sit and watch it. On TV it looks better, too. It has all the special effects and the creatures look better. It makes you think it really could happen in the future.'

'You can actually see them doing it all, landing on the moon or the planets, you can see it happen.'

Documentary

The news and documentary side of television is more obviously a source of education for the young and also an example of the blurred lines between fantasy and reality.

The wildlife and science programmes such as 'World About Us', 'Life on Earth', 'Horizon', 'Tomorrow's World', etc. are all direct extensions of school lessons but more up to date and better presented. Because television caters for such a mass market, it has become very good at mass education by the use of visual aids, film, presentation etc. – techniques and facilities outside the scope of school teachers. Television is also good at reducing the facts to easily understood basics. The young rate many of these programmes among their favourites which shows that when given a free choice they are serious about learning, they're not only interested in fun and thrillers.

The science programmes often deal with new technology, of particular interest to the young. They like to know what is happening and what are the latest innovations. They take it for granted that scientists are continually developing new or better equipment and they have an underlying belief that sooner or later anything is possible. School, though, tends to be far behind in these matters, so the young rely on television for up-to-date information.

The news is vitally important to adults but less so to the young. They enjoy news programmes but not really the news itself. It's not surprising really, as school children have no power or control in terms of newsworthy events. They can't vote, they are not consumers in the eyes of industry, they have practically no legal rights, so why should they be concerned by what is happening in the world? Also, 'the world' is a difficult thought to grasp for a teenager who has barely been outside his or her home town. Sarah at twelve feels much more at home with the local news items on 'Nationwide' or 'Thames at Six' because they deal with an environment she knows and understands: ' "Nationwide" is good. They do all sorts of things, ghosts, pop, UFOs, all different things. It's for children as well as adults and they have a man playing the piano who sings about the news.' For Sarah, 'Nationwide' is like a popular newspaper such as the *Daily Mail*, whilst the main news represents *The Times*, and she would never read the latter. 'Nationwide', or any other news magazine, rarely deals with the serious, heavy subjects such as war, civil unrest and international politics, and Sarah feels more comfortable with it.

News frequently deals with death – whether in the form of war, murder or natural disasters. 'I don't really like it because it's nearly all fighting.' Even the sixteen-year-olds were worried about death and got upset to see newsreels where people are involved in any real physical violence. 'I love John Craven's newsround but when I see two more people killed in Rhodesia I nearly want to cry. I feel so sorry for them and I get upset.' They realized newsreels show the reality; these were reporters telling you what was happening, the people killed weren't just actors who would be seen next week in another TV film playing a different part, they were real people. The kids didn't know how to deal with this.

Likewise, 'Panorama' was given a general thumbs down. While death upset them, shook their foundations, politics just bored them: 'I don't like "Panorama", it's boring, it's all about this country, rising prices and politics. It's boring for children. It probably won't be in five or six years time when I'm an adult and have to look after myself.'

Fifteen-year-old Andy was very serious about school and working hard to get his O levels, but his comments about 'Panorama' echoed a general feeling amongst other teenagers. They have no say in the way the country is run; they don't understand what politicians talk about and they can do nothing about the rising prices.

'Politics on television is so boring I go out. I don't know why they have it on really.'

Anyway Mum and Dad look after you so you don't have to worry. At this age they have no concept of the future. O levels maybe, but 'adulthood' is almost a mythical state of mind to be achieved in years to come.

Some documentaries were liked, but much depended upon the subject. Frequently they fitted into the sociology classes taught in many comprehensives. In the social sciences teachers seemed more inclined to use television as an extension of the classroom. 'I watched a programme on the National Front; we were doing Race in social studies so the teacher told us to watch it.'

Sometimes though they had problems seeing the difference between documentary and documentary-style drama because they used the same techniques and style of filming. It could be confusing. One inconsistency was noticed by Simon, and it worried him:

'In those wild life programmes you see buffalo dying and you'd think the cameraman would go up and help them – but I suppose they're not allowed to.'

Music

'Top of the Pops' is one of the most popular programmes with the young. It is not thought perfect, but it is the best of its kind on television. Pop music is largely neglected on television. Vision is important because the fans need to know how the bands look, how they move, how the audience is dressed and the way they dance. Very few in this age group can afford to go to live concerts, certainly not on a regular basis, so television is the only way to actually see a group perform. Joanne watches 'Top of the Pops' regularly every week without fail:

'I watch it to keep in touch with what sort of music is in now and it's a chance to see the group, to know what they're like, which you don't know if you only listen to them. It's good to see whether or not they're nice looking and what clothes they wear.'

The serious music fan, however, criticized the programme

because it did not cater for minority tastes in music. There were other music programmes such as 'The Old Grey Whistle Test' or 'Rock Goes to College' but these were on late at night and often catered for an older esoteric taste. The teenagers wanted to see more music programmes.

Sports and romance

All these programmes are watched and enjoyed by both boys and girls alike. Sport and love stories, however, tend to have a more specialized following. Generally, sport programmes mean the television football and cricket matches. All the males in the family monopolize the telly for 'Match of the Day' etc. 'My dad and my brothers take over the colour telly and my mum and me have to go out in the kitchen in the cold with the black and white.' But girls are interested in sports such as athletics, swimming, skating, and particularly, gymnastics.

Teenage girls love romance. Beverly watches all the love stories on television as well as buying romantic magazines. She explained what she got out of them:

'I feel I want to take the girl's place and have a nice young man and a lot of money. I love the way they look at each other and kiss, and they are so very close they can't bear to be apart. Holding each other in their arms and not really needing words to say anything ... having a nice relationship, being able to talk to each other.'

It was hard to believe that Beverly was also a tomboy who played football with the boys.

One of the most important aspects of television is that it's there in the home and it's free. It provides instant entertainment and new experiences, and one of the reasons school holidays can be boring is that often there aren't any good programmes on during the day. It is something to do in the evenings.

Radio

All the other media pale into insignificance compared with television. 'I can't get used to it after television.' The young see the radio as a background medium, something to play music. The majority of those we talked to had their own radios and when they woke up in the morning, on went the radio.

It seems as though they can't stand silence. They need to have noise around them, and that is the main use of the radio. They have it on when they're getting ready for school, washing, dressing eating breakfast: 'I only listen to the radio in the mornings. I don't really listen though, it's just incidental, in the background when I'm getting ready for school.' Many of those who took their homework seriously would switch on the radio when they got home: 'It helps me concentrate on my homework.' 'It puts my mind at rest when I'm doing my homework.' Silence appears to be distracting. Many, however, would just come home from school and switch on the telly and listen to that for the rest of the evening. The trouble with radio is that there are no pictures and too many words: 'I get bored listening to the radio – it's all talking.' 'I don't like talking. I don't find it very interesting.'

They need the visuals to bring the words to life.

Although they are derogatory about the radio, they do like to listen to the music on the breakfast shows and they all listen to the Hit Parade shows every week; it keeps them up to date. At school they discuss what is happening in the charts and it gives an indication of what is going on in the music world. It is vital information that no one can afford to be without and they frequently tape it so they can listen again. But the charts only play established hits. Those who really care about music would listen to the late-night record shows such as John Peel, to find out the 'news' items in the music business, to pick up on trends and to hear new bands play. Disc jockeys such as John Peel are a source of information about trends in music and also cater for a wide range of esoteric tastes that would not be heard on the 'mass market' music programmes. John Peel's 'talk' is news but the talk of most programme presenters is dull and boring: 'They say nothing, so why don't they just play the records?' Their allegiances go with whichever radio station plays the best music – in their opinion. But there are always constant interruptions on the radio, it caters for the adult obsession with the news. 'It's bad enough listening to news on the television without it being on the radio all day,' and on commercial radio there are the adverts too.

Radio is a solitary medium and it has most appeal for those who like to be on their own. Those girls and boys who were beginning to reject the family would often go to their bedroom and listen to the radio until the early hours of the morning. They were starting to be independent. For sports enthusiasts it also offers a better coverage of local football matches. But overall, it tends to have little appeal for the young and always seems second best: 'If I'm bored with my tape recorder I can play with the radio.'

It was of limited interest for this age group and while mornings are when most of them listen, if breakfast time TV is introduced they will resort to the more exciting, visual medium of the television.

The printed word
Magazines, books and newspapers also suffer badly in comparison with television.

Newspapers can be quickly dismissed: 'If you listen to the news on the telly then there's no point reading newspapers.' Although a newspaper does have its uses:

'It tells you what programmes are on and what time.'

'I look at sport and to see how many bits are in there today ... the one yesterday was really good.'

'I always turn to Snoopy – he's my favourite.'

Newspapers are glanced at if they are in the home but it is only the more spectacular articles or features that the kids read. News is more interestingly reported on television and it has the benefit of 'live' reporting. Reading ability does vary, and while the *Sun* and *Mirror* were easy to read, the brighter kids like Paul realized their banality:

'They can be boring; you get things about Prince Charles playing polo in the headlines, which is stupid, and then half-way through they've got a little article squeezed in about a woman stabbed to death.'

But on the other hand *The Times* wasn't ideal: 'There's too much to read, it's all stories and it's very serious.'

Books seem to suffer as a result of this attitude to words and also the varying standards of literacy. Maybe teenagers will grow into books when they become disenchanted with television, but at the moment they are part of an increasingly visual society. They want all their messages to be visual, or at least have a high picture content. They seemed to get no thrill out of books and associate them mainly with school.

Joanne's point of view is common:

'I read books at school; you have to. But actually I'd rather read a comic. I do sometimes pick up a book but then I put it down after a while.'

The reason for Joanne's putting down the book is mainly one of time. Time is precious, they are always dashing around doing things, they find it hard to sit still, they want to be active. The trouble with books is that they take time to read and they are passive. Comic books or annuals are all right because there is no long story to follow, but a novel demands time to become engrossed and involved in the story. 'It's stupid, you need to sit around all the time reading in order to follow the story.' When they were younger and went to bed earlier they were allowed to read for half an hour before going to sleep but now they were staying up later and watching all the exciting adult programmes on telly.

Maybe the visual images on television are making their imaginations lazy, they're relying on the director to do it all for them: 'I read books because they're exciting, but I don't like reading. I can't always follow mysteries and I can't picture things in my mind like the telly has.' Quite a few of the teenagers experienced difficulties following the plot in a book. This could be due to comprehension and reading problems or maybe television has become too good at simplifying ideas so they don't have to think too hard, just enjoy it.

Money is a problem with books – they tend to cost too much for pocket money to allow, so are out of reach. School and public libraries are used by some and there is also a fair amount of swapping of paperbacks, particularly sensational ones, between friends at school. Books are sometimes used as reference material – Kevin was mad about gangsters and got books out of the library on Al Capone, and Tina was always up to date in fashion and would use books to research into past fashions and to check out authenticity of styles.

For Joanne and many of her age group, one of the main failings of books is: 'They're not up to date.' And that is a problem when compared to the immediacy of television or radio. The young want to know what is happening now.

Magazines and comics manage to reflect a fairly good picture of teenage interests. They come out regularly and they can be afforded, although the really smart kids get them put on the paper bill and Mum pays. There was a great deal of variety in what they read, and individuals would buy for themselves magazines that suited their own particular interests and reading skills. Words are less of a problem in comics and magazines because the stories are shorter and they have pictures to illustrate them.

Boys and girls of all ages love fun comics like the *Beano*. They are cheap and a good laugh. The humour is ageless and really the same style as their favourite comedy series such as 'Fawlty Towers' or 'Kenny Everett'. Expensive, glossy magazines are rarely bought, although frequently swapped and borrowed.

The kids tended to criticize television, radio, books and films because they felt generally that they were not aimed sufficiently at the adolescent age group. However magazines didn't have this problem. The music enthusiast can read *New Musical Express* or *Sounds* and find out what is happening:

'I'm a Heavy Metal fan and *Sounds* tells you about the concerts and whether it's worth going to see them.'

'I've been buying *NME* because Selector have an album and a single coming out, and they had a page on that telling you about them and what the group are like.'

'They tell you what's happening.'

Many of the kids wanted to learn the words from all the latest hits. Then they could sing along with the songs on the radio or make up their own groups. So magazines that included chart song words were popular.

Boys with hobbies or particular interests could get specialist magazines. Simon was mad on hot rods and he was always designing cars he would like to make one day, so he bought

Street Car to give him some ideas. Kevin made Airfix models so he had the monthly magazine delivered.

Adolescents are shy, self-conscious and fascinated by sex. Magazines must be the only medium that actually helps them with their personal problems and answers the questions they are too embarrassed to ask their parents and too ignorant to help each other out with. Girls avidly read the problem pages even though they appeared to be scornful of them at first:

'I read them all the time ... I read them for a laugh, I read them out loud to other people. You get things like "Can I catch VD by sitting on a toilet seat?" ... stupid!'

Michelle might say 'stupid' but that was the sort of question she really wanted answers to. She was more sophisticated, but still relied on the problem page of her mum's magazine to let her into some of the secrets of adults:

'My boy-friend, he's always asking me to have sex and I've said no and I really want to – all that jam is stupid. If you read *Woman's Own*, at least they're older and you can find out more from them.'

Not all the problems were about sex. Beverly liked *Jackie* for its answers to problems: 'There's some good things in it; it explains what to do if you've got a spot on your nose or if your hair needs washing, it helps to make you feel better, it has some good ideas of things that will help you.'

When the boys got the chance they read the problem pages too. They had questions about sex and personal problems and they were even more shy than the girls to ask for help although they wouldn't admit to it. Girls' magazines also gave them an insight into what girls thought of boys, how they felt about sex, what periods are, etc. Girls had a safe, secure place to read about problems. The answers were always sensible and helpful – a bit like Mum's. In practice, though, most boys seem to learn about sex from the soft porn magazines. Even eleven and twelve-year-olds had access to the girlie magazines. Once again the school playground was the main place for them to be swapped and looked at:

'I think all kids like *Mayfair*. If a kid brings one into school he'd soon get thirty kids gathered round.'

There was a lot of status attached to owning porn magazines, but Andy showing off his 'experience' to the rest of the group, felt he had grown out of them – at fifteen:

'I wouldn't buy them any more now; I wouldn't waste my money. When I was about twelve, at puberty and all that sort of stuff, I wanted to read them. Now I wouldn't bother. It depends on what your sex life is like at the moment. If it's good you don't want to read it 'cause you're getting it all ... it's a bit boring after you've read a few because you're substituting aren't you?'

The girls at mixed schools were aware of the playground dealing in dirty magazines but they disapproved. Not surprisingly since they were so uptight about their own bodies: 'I don't mind naked women by a swimming pool but the women in those magazines are disgusting, horrible, they should be banned.'

Girls disapproved of such blatant sex but they didn't mind romance – that was different. Love stories were an escape into a fantasy world, the heroines never had to decide whether or not to sleep with their boy-friends or what to do about a spot. Some of the others, though, did deal with real life situations. Beverly had been helped in coming to terms with her family life: 'I really enjoyed the story about the girl who was adopted and the old sister is a bit hard and jealous. I feel sorry for the girl, I wouldn't want to be adopted and feel left out ... how hard it must be to have no mother or no parents ... when I was little I used to be jealous, and my mum used to get bothered by my first dad, so I've seen a lot of it.'

Fashion is an important element of girls' magazines. It shows them where to buy fashions and how much they cost. Apart from shop windows, magazines were seen to be the best guide to fashions.

The kids had their favourite magazines and comics but they did not always have the money to buy them. So they would swap them around at school as well as reading whatever was on hand at home. While a thirteen-year-old girl might prefer to read *Jackie* she is likely to end up a regular reader of *Woman's Own* because that is what her mum buys, and that would provide a source for many of her ideas.

Magazines are more 'fun' than books and newspapers. They are more visually stimulating, and they have added variety with the range of features, stories and articles. But they still use the written word and rely on reading ability. The kids' reticence at getting involved with reading and literature might suggest the youth of today are becoming illiterate, but they can express their thoughts and ideas very well, once they start talking. Television (and radio) does seem to have made them more articulate.

Films

Cinema hardly featured in the comments of the kids we talked to because 'It costs two quid these days and you've got your bus fare into town,' and 'all the films are either Us or As, which are for kids, or if they're any good they're an X.' The conversations were dominated by discussions of X films, not particularly because of their merit, but because they were forbidden fruit. The younger the boy or girl the greater the status achieved by getting into an X. How sorry one is for the small fifteen-year-old who never looks his age, never mind eighteen:

'I know kids that have got into X's. They're only a little bit taller than me and they've gone to see films like *Alien* and *Roller Ball*.'

Beverly managed though by devious methods:

'I really wanted to see *The Bitch*, so they opened the toilet window and pulled me through.'

The young did not understand why there was this censorship of films. They presumed it was due to violence and swearing but they heard that on the streets and saw violence as television.

'There's a lot of X's about and the only reason is because there's a lot of swearing in them ... but you don't take any notice, you hear more swearing at school.'

'I've seen *The Godfather* on telly and "The Sweeney" is violent but you don't go out and kick someone just because you've seen it on the telly.'

They also claimed to have seen more explicit sex on television than in the cinema.

Science fiction films are popular partly because this new wave of special effect space films could only be seen at the cinema, but also because they're much more dramatic on the big screen, as also are horror films. The high standard of special effects made fantasy so much more wonderful amongst the older boys and girls that there was a certain kudos in being the first to see a new film, particularly one that received a bit of publicity. But the problem with teenagers and the cinema is that very few films seem to cater to them, as with the other media.

'We're at a difficult age. Really it's all for children or adults; there's not much in between.'

The films that came nearest to meeting their needs were those that had music in them:

'Music makes them more interesting ... we all went to see *The Great Rock 'n Roll Swindle*, and that was great, really funny. Johnny Rotten was outrageous and the Rock'n Roll scene was really smart. First of all he's singing "My Way" and then he goes Punk.'

But again the younger music fan is prohibited from much.

'I'd like to see *Quadrophenia*, but that was an AA. Everyone was talking about it, and I really wanted to see what it was all about ... all the children that had seen it were taller than me ... *Breaking Glass* is meant to be good, too, but that's an X. My friend said the music was really good, and I was jealous.'

Advertising

They see advertising as not only selling products but also as a form of entertainment. A television commercial for Heineken, Guinness or a Hamlet cigar can be just as funny as the comedy programme on before the break, and Benson and Hedges posters have become part of the landscape. More than eight out of ten of the kids we talked to agreed that television commercials are often fun to watch. But commercials have to stand up to the same criteria as the programmes themselves:

'There's nothing as bad as a boring advert.'

'I hate those ones that never look professional.'

The young seem more prepared to accept advertising as a

fact of life; they're not antagonistic like their parents but take it for granted:

'Advertising is everywhere, everywhere you turn, magazines, it's on bill boards, papers, perfumes, shavers, speed-rolling – it's all over the place, on trains, buses and even in comics.'

So what the media does for the young is give them ideas and information. But it depends on the kids being totally passive. It is a one-way system and they give no feedback. If they could, it would definitely be, 'Give us more to suit our own interests.'

10 The teenage consumer

Everything costs

Half-past three on Saturday afternoon and Andy is at a loose end. He spent this morning mucking about down town with his mates, bought himself some fish and chips and came back home. Simon and his friends are going to watch the Arsenal match. Andy was going to go too, but while they were checking out Halfords earlier on, he found that the metallic blue paint he'd been waiting for had just come in, so he bought that instead. He's doing up his old racer so that next year, if there's enough money in the building society, he can afford to buy a motor bike. Should he start spraying the bike now? No, he needs it tonight. He's going to the disco on the new estate and if he doesn't have his bike, it'll cost him 70p in bus fares. He's got £2.80 in his pocket, the disco will cost £1 to get in and drinks will be 75p on top of that, if he sticks to shandy. That leaves him £1.05 for the rest of the week (and he promised Mum he would save 50p as a regular thing). It would be nice to have a packet of fags tonight to show the gang he's still one step ahead. Should he get those or should he save the 56p in case he wants to buy a drink for a girl tonight? He did see Joan Murser outside Jean Machine this morning, and she said she might be going. He may try and ask her out . . . of course, if she agrees to go to the pictures, she'll have to pay for herself. Girls are always trying to exploit blokes these days. Perhaps he should have saved the £1 Mum gave him for the fish and chips, but he was hungry and everyone else was getting them. At least he persuaded Mum to get him the right parka for his birthday, so he'll look good tonight. He really wanted the Mod boots as well, but she wouldn't budge. He'll have to save up for those himself, but he's not going to have anything left to save this week. The boots are £19.95, so if he saves 50p a week, it'll take him forty weeks to get them. But by then, Mod might not be in fashion any more. At least the 'I hate Skinheads' badge only cost 25p, so people will know he's a Mod even if he hasn't got the boots. But if he saves up for the boots, how's he going to get enough together for the motor bike? He'll probably have to wait until he's got a proper job; he'll never get it with just a paper round. Andy slumps in front of the telly. The Arsenal match is on. At least it's free!

All the young people we talked to spend a lot of their time out on the streets – looking. They look at people and they look at shop windows and this gives them lots of ideas about how to spend their money:

'When I go into Manchester there's so much there, I just like to look, see what's around, see the sales, all the new fashions, see what things are coming out, then if you see something you like you can start saving up.'

'Brent Cross – you can walk around it for ever and ever, see what they've got, just look in windows.'

'We just have a look around, go to the café upstairs, play on the TV games.'

'You get ideas from seeing people walking around. If they look good you try and copy them.'

Joanne and Debbie are parked at the Boots' perfume counter, spraying on the testers. Joanne has run out of skin to spray them on. Lovingly she decides which one she wants, puts it back on the counter and resolves to get Mum to pass the name on to Aunty. At £3.25 that will have to be a birthday present. On to the cosmetics. Look at the eyeshadows and the nail varnish. She doesn't need lipstick, because she's still got some and she doesn't use a lot, but she would *love* some green eyeshadow to match her new T-shirt. Charlie, Revlon, Max Factor, Estée Lauder, Mary Quant. She soaks up the smiling, confident models, the luxury, the sophistication, but makes for Miners, Rimmel and Boots 17 to begin an exhaustive evaluation of the price tags. There's glamour in a Mary Quant eye pallette, but if she buys a 60p eyeshadow from Rimmel, then she can afford the mascara to go with it as well.

Chelsea Girl is the next stop – rows of pencil skirts, rainbow

T-shirts, glittering lights. This skirt is just like the one in *Jackie* last week and she could get it for £6.99. She gets £2.40 a week with her baby sitting money, so possibly she could save enough in four weeks to buy it. But then has she got anything to go with it? Perhaps her sister would lend her the yellow sweat-shirt now that she doesn't wear it so much ... if she saves for the skirt, would her mother give her the money for swimming? There's a girl in her class, who gets £5 a week and her mother pays for riding lessons and ice skating as well. But it's not going to be easy for Joanne to save because her nan's birthday is this month and it's Mother's Day after that. She won't be able to get the skirt until just before she goes on holiday. Will it be the right thing for Spain?

Debbie is calling her over to the jewellery stand. The shop girl looks young, so they try on some of the earrings. Debbie decides to buy a pair with purple plastic feathers on. Joanne is torn between the same pair in green and a pair of green socks, which she needs to go with her jeans and T-shirt. She is tempted to slip the earrings into her pocket ... still, perhaps she could make some feathered earrings at home. She's got a pair she doesn't like any more and her brother's got an old Indian headdress!

The girl behind the counter doesn't look much older than she is. In just over a year's time Joanne plans to get a part-time job herself. Think of the clothes she could buy with £8 a week – that's over three times as much as she's getting now. She and Debbie go back to Debbie's place to experiment with their new make-up. She'd like to go to the Roller Disco tonight, but she and Mike can't really afford it, so they'll probably go for a long walk instead. At least it's free!

David, twelve, collects stickers, buys sweets, reads the *Beano* and thirsts after a new pair of football boots, all on £1.25 a week. Sarah, twelve, wants a tape to record the new Blondie album, some marker pens, depends on her weekly copy of *Jackie*, and is saving for a pair of high heels and a rabbit on £1.35 a week.

Harry, sixteen, has to finance eating out, record albums, beer, clothes, even contraceptives out of £4.10 a week, and

Michelle, sixteen, covets shoes, the odd can of Coke, hair colour, clothes, make-up and concerts on £3.85.

Imagine how you'd feel if you had £25 a week to cover everything bar food and mortgage, and a normal dress cost £150, beer cost £3.50 a pint, a packet of cigarettes cost £6.25 and the bus fare into town and back came to £7. Pretty soon a Mars bar at £2.50 and a copy of *Jackie* at £1.40 start looking like very good value.

It means that everything Joanne buys is deeply pondered and precisely accounted for. An impulse purchase might be a disaster, 'like a pair of earrings, then you'll regret you've spent it'. If you live on £2.35 a week, then riding on the roundabouts means giving up on the swings. The 60p which buys you a packet of cigarettes is not going to buy you a bottle of nail varnish as well.

It means that when Simon spends a fifth of his income on a badge saying 'I'm Mummy's little angel', that badge must express to the world exactly what he wants to say about himself. It mustn't go rusty and must last until he has got tired of it.

It means that when Harry offers round a packet of fags which cost an eighth of all the money he has, then the gesture assumes a greater significance than if you or I were to do it.

There's always daydreaming. Frances and her best friend are only twelve and have hardly any money for clothes but they like to talk and dream about the clothes they would like to buy. Their solution to this is 'dressing up': 'My dad used to take us into Slough and we'd go to C & A and then we'd take clothes off the rack and go into the changing room, try them all on and walk up and down in front of the mirror. Then we'd take them back, get another lot and keep on doing it.'

I feel humble and slightly guilty that Michelle admires my two-tone shirt so fervently, when I know it is only one of many hanging in my wardrobe. When I buy a shirt, I don't appreciate it nearly as much as she does. I begin to see how tempting it must be to nick something. It occurs to me that one reason teenage boys might not bother to use contraceptives is that they cost too much. I see suddenly how seductive gambling must be, with its promise of huge rewards: 'Something to do, a chance you can win, like that bloke who won the pools!'

Purse strings/Apron strings?

But money does more for you than giving you the items you fancy. Money also gives you the freedom to be what you want to be. Sarah understands the trade-off:

'With money, you get more things and you can go and buy your *own* things. If you haven't you just wear the same things all the time.'

Harry's mum is middle class and respectable. She's never going to finance the black leather, razor blades, chains, earrings and green hairdye he needs for a Punk outfit. Unless he can hustle up some funds of his own the option of being a full-blooded Punk just isn't open to him. If Beverly always depends on her mum for money to go to the pictures, then she's going to be stuck when Mum withholds the cash, because she doesn't approve of the latest boy-friend.

Very few mums hand over the money and give their children free choice, and if they do they want to be sure what they are paying for:

'If I do see something and I don't want to take my mum to town, I'll try and find something like it in a book and she says whether or not she approves – but she usually comes with me and makes me try it on again.'

'If Mum's seen it she'll give me the money, but if I don't give her a good description she'll come with me.'

Mums seem to have more difficulty with boys' clothes and a strong-minded teenager like David is able to browbeat his mum into giving him the money:

'She's got no idea, so I go out buying on my own. She gives me the money. If I left it to her she'd get it wrong; it would be the wrong size or the wrong colour.'

The best solution is to save up and buy it yourself then there are no rows or complaints: 'I save up my money and then I can get what I want.'

There's also another spin-off. Managing money so you can get what you want isn't play acting in the way that being in the fashion is play acting. It is a real skill. If Joanne can make £3.25 a week stretch to a Pretenders' album, a new skirt and a trip to the cinema, then when she gets paid £50 a week she'll be able to pay the mortgage, eat out on Saturdays and take a holiday in Florida. No one has to manage on as little money as the teenager who is still at school.

Doling out money is the action of a parent to a child, whether it is the government or Mum at home. It is not the action of equal to equal. There are always hidden sanctions because the person with the money has the power. The worker on the dole feels less of a man, the housewife without her own income feels she has fewer rights and the teenager who accepts hand-outs remains a child until he's earned the money to go out and do something Mum doesn't approve of.

Still, no one has to prove that money buys independence to the teenagers I talked to. They are too busy hustling.

Consider Harry's position: 'From the way I like to live I don't get enough!' He wants the money so he can be a proper teenager. Rich widows worry about what to spend their money on, fathers of families worry about how to keep their money safe, teenagers worry about how to maximize the amount coming in – I admire their ingenuity.

Here are the rules for getting as much as you can:

1 Get Mum to buy whatever she'll agree to.
2 Get yourself a part time job, preferably one which doesn't take up all your free time.
3 Publicize what you want for Christmas and birthday and make sure Auntie Susan gives you money and not a book token.
4 Be around when generous relatives come to visit.

Anything lying around the house is fair game – biscuits, beer, moisturizing cream, Dad's old shirts, Mum's *Woman's Own*. Andy can experiment with his sister's spot cream without it costing him a penny. If Michelle can last out until she gets home, she can drink the family Coca-Cola instead of spending 25p in town on a can of her own.

Clothes are the worst problem; they are too expensive to buy without Mum's help, but Mum's idea of how you should look is much too conservative. 'I need the money to buy my own clothes – fashionable clothes,' says Michelle. 'My mum

166

will buy me, say, one pair of shoes a year. The rest I have to buy for myself.'

They let Mum buy what they need for school and messing about at home and concentrate their own funds on fashion.

What Mum buys is what Mum approves of, but all Mums realize that they can't clip their children's wings altogether. Mums provide regular cash without strings attached. Each family manages it a different way.

Beverly (13): 'Well, we get 10p every morning. When it's youth club night, we get 20p for a night even if we haven't used up our other lot Fridays. We get 30p in the morning to go to school and 50p of a night off my mum when I come home from school.'

Ian (13): '£1.50 I get given and my dad puts 50p away a week for me.'

Judy (15): 'My mum buys all my clothes and everything, but I don't get pocket money. If I want some money to go out, she pays for it, but I don't get a fixed rate of pocket money.'

Harry (16): 'When I'm at school, I get £1.50 a week bus fares. I work with my dad, he's a joiner, and I get £3 and £2 pocket money.'

Michelle (16): 'I get £13.50 a month clothes' allowance, and Dad gives me some money if I need it, you know. I say to Dad "Lend me a few quid," and he'll give me like a fiver, so at least I've got money to go out.'

If you're a girl, you're more likely to wangle money out of your parents. If you're a boy, you're more likely to have fixed pocket money and be looking around for a way to make more. Money is money, whatever it is earmarked for. If Mum gives you £1 a week for school dinners and £2.30 for bus fares, then if you can cadge a lift and go hungry, you've made £3.30 to spend on better things. Simon's priorities would make Mum shudder: 'I get 35p dinner money which goes on my cigarettes. I don't eat dinner and I get £1.50 to £2.

Jobs

One in three teenagers still at school has got a formal part-time job.

Let's see what that means.

Boys lead more independent lives than girls do, they're out of the house more, and they *can't* ask Mum for money. Anyone can see that Mum's reaction is going to be different when Beverly, thirteen, asks for 70p to go ice-skating from when Ian, thirteen, asks for 70p for a copy of *Men Only*. Roughly twice as many boys as girls have part-time jobs.

When they are Simon and Sarah's age, kids think of themselves as children and children don't expect to have to work for a living. Less than one in ten have a job. By the time Ian and Beverly have hit thirteen, Ian knows he's going to need cash to impress his friends, because at 4 ft 9 in his size isn't going to do it. But Beverly still depends on Mum, she lacks confidence to go out and hustle. At 13 and 14, two and a half times as many boys as girls have fixed themselves up with a part-time job. But by the age of 16, like Michelle and Beverly, the girls have caught up. They want their independence too and they need the clothes. They also find that they're expected to pay for themselves when they go out. Two girls in every five and more than half the boys are working part-time. They don't all like it, either. 'Money isn't everything is it? I want my Saturdays; it's the only time I get free,' says Michelle, but once you've tasted the rewards, there's no turning back: 'I wouldn't work for pleasure,' says Andy ruefully, 'everybody hates it, but the money comes in. You can go out and enjoy yourself.' They are tackling every job you can think of. They will work for the local newsagent, for their mum's company, in a shop, for their brother, for the Squash Club. Good jobs are precious, as one person grows out of a job, another steps into it. Trafficking in jobs goes on at school and in the family.

Michelle: 'I had to fight for that job. When my sister ran away, she said that I could have it.'

Ian: 'I wash this lady's car that my brother used to wash, that's 70p – £1 odd.'

Look what the boys are up to:

'I do little jobs, like drawing posters for the Squash Club.'

'I get £1.50 off the milk round.'

'I get £6.25, stacking shelves.'

'I go out and clean the car, or weed the garden, or do the wiping up for about 10p, or make the tea when it's not my turn.'

'I have £4 because of my paper round.'

'I deliver leaflets for an estate agent. It's supposed to be 80p an hour, which is a bit slave labour.'

'My mum used to be an invoice clerk, and I used to help out in the holidays. Pretty easy work. I got five quid for working three mornings.'

'Army cadets will give you £120 to go for two weeks' camping.'

'I worked last summer holidays on a building site. I didn't get bad money, but I cut my hands so I didn't go again.'

'Quite a few kids get £10 just working in a green grocer – not delivery, just working.'

And the girls:

'I baby sit regularly. I get £1 if I don't baby sit and £2 if I do.'

'I work for my mum.'

'I work at Selfridges.'

'I had a job in the toy shop up the road. I packed that up. Then I worked in a shop in Putney. I packed that up because of the money. I mean I got £6 a week for a day!'

'My brother gives me money for cleaning his football boots.'

'I used to get £6 a week for a paper round but it was an hour a day, every morning at six.'

'I did work from 6.30 to 8.30 where my brother works. I can't sell anything, but I put things back on the shelves, as I know where they go.'

What with school and homework there isn't a lot of time left for working, but they manage it. Most popular are part-time weekday jobs, which don't encroach on the weekend. When they're thirteen, any money seems a lot, but by the time they reach sixteen they know what is a decent wage, and are already beginning to voice resentment, if they think they are being exploited.

Shopping

The kids spend most of their money buying things, but how do they know which shops they should go to? This was a difficult question to answer but it turned out to be the result of a combination of factors. Because they're always hanging around on the 'streets' they see the shop windows and see who shops there so they know what is available for what sort of person. The customers help them to assess whether it is likely to be 'their' type of shop and word of mouth is important too. They talk a lot to each other about what they buy and are planning to buy so their school friends offer helpful advice. Where clothes and fashion items are concerned they are certainly going to shop in places that cater for their particular style.

'I don't know how you tell really, just walk around, when you're walking you take a note of what they've got ... people at school tell you, you get to know ... shop windows.'

'Just look and see what's around.'

'I ask people who look good where they get their clothes.'

Where are the best places to shop? Firstly it's worth explaining what a teenager means by 'shopping'. They may eventually make a purchase, but most of the time they're just looking around, sizing up one thing against another, asking for their mates' opinions, deciding just how much they want to buy it. It all goes back to their lack of money – they have to make sure what they buy is right. They also get a lot of pleasure first by simply browsing around shops – looking at toiletries, magazines, books, stationery, records, fashion accessories, models, kits, toys, games, sweets etc. The kids felt free to poke around, see what was for sale, try out the testers, browse without being harassed and hustled: 'It's trendy to go to a place like Virgin Records on a Saturday morning – all the punks sit around outside so I really enjoy going there – it's just the getting over the fear of going through the door ...'

The young like the shops that leave them free to browse. The multiple chain stores like Boots, Woolworth's, W. H. Smith were universally popular because they were large and spacious. The goods were all well displayed and accessible and the overall atmosphere of the store was anonymous.

Freedom was also required in fashion shops. They didn't want assistants coming up to them all the time, they just wanted to look at the clothes in peace. They would choose their clothes shops by the style of the clothes and the price range of the goods and the grapevine played a large role in determining which shop they visited. Record shops were very popular and were a regular Saturday afternoon haunt for many of the kids. They were often more of a club than a shop and everyone went there not only to hear music and to glean information from the record sleeves but also to see what everyone was wearing and what they were doing. Sports shops were popular with the boys, so were toy model and joke shops.

Simon liked cameras and studied all the photographic shop windows in an attempt to learn about cameras and plan his eventual purchase. Being so knowledgeable also gave him a degree of status in his gang at school: 'I look at lenses and cameras I can't afford. I make out I'm interested and say thank you and walk out of the shop.' Beverly and her friends couldn't pass a jeweller's without going to look at the engagement rings. 'When we don't know what to do we go and look in Samuels and look at all those diamond rings. I know just the one I want!'

Marks and Spencer must be the epitome of everything young people hate about shops:

'Every time your mum wants something it's always down to Marks and Spencer's, they're bound to have it there ... that's the trouble. They've always got it; doesn't matter what size or shape, we're having it.'

'They're cheap, it always seems as though you haven't gone to any trouble getting it, it's like just anything will do.'

'It's for married men and they're not fashion conscious are they? They'd just walk into Marks and get what they want, like our mums do ... we prefer proper clothes shops, but then they've got no sense of fashion.'

'There's only a little bit for children, most of it is either food or adults' stuff. You see all these cut price girdles and women's under-pants just laying there – things like that, nothing for children.'

Atmosphere

'The minute you walk in with your mates they watch you.'

Apart from all the unfashionable associations, what all the kids I talked to hated most about M & S was being watched all the time. They made the same comment about other stores they disliked such as department stores:

'They keep an eye on you in case you're going to swipe something.'

'I hate those stores like Selfridges, they always think we're going to nick something, they think kids are always thieving.'

'You get a trail because they think you're going to nick something, they follow you all over the place.'

'You can see all the assistants keeping an eye on you just 'cause you're young ... they watch you all the time.'

It's not surprising they felt distinctly uncomfortable and edgy. On the surface they may seem full of bravado, but underneath they're a quivering mass of nerves and to be constantly watched made them more embarrassed and shy than ever, as well as creating a gulf between them and adults.

Sometimes they were challenged, as happened to Debbie and her friends at the Brent Cross Shopping Centre:

'We are looking round the shops after school and this bloke who'd been trailing us comes over and says what's under your jacket? – we were just mucking around and it was funny really ... but it was embarrassing too, everybody was looking.'

Beverly was terrified about wrongful arrest: 'When you go shopping they've got them tellys, that annoys me, they're just looking at you all the time, you feel really funny ... Suppose you had something in your purse and you didn't want anyone else to see, or suppose you'd got Polos from another shop and you get one out to eat and they think you've nicked

172

'... I hate it when I just reach my hand in my pocket to put my watch on or something like that and people think you're shoplifting. It happened to my auntie once, they took her back into this room and said she'd been shoplifting. She wasn't and she was quite old and got really upset about it.'

The kids were aware there was a lot of shoplifting going on. They had seen people do it and a few had even done it themselves:

'You see people shoving things in their pockets right in front of those cameras ... and when I went into Lewis's at Christmas there was a man there just filling a shopping bag full of socks and pants, just doing it in front of everybody.'

'I went in with my friend's brother once and he was nicking everything he could get his hands on ... and he got away with it.'

'I've nicked bars of chocolate from shops, things like that ... just walked out with something in my pocket.'

'I haven't been in a shop for the intent purpose of nicking ... you just get fed up waiting there so you put it in your pocket and walk out.'

Morally, they do not object to stealing from a shop but they are worried by the police who are a deterrent. Simon has nicked small things from shops but felt he was entitled to a second chance if caught.

So, they realized why they were watched in shops but nevertheless they hated it. Not surprisingly, therefore, their favourite shops were the ones which left them free to wander around without the heavy looks or the obvious store detectives:

'They'll help you without being pushy, they let you look after yourself without keeping on, "Can I help you?" all the time. I prefer it when I say "Can you help me?" and they're nice about it and they don't force you into things.'

The young people I talked with were astonishingly perceptive about shop assistants – they didn't miss anything. They knew what they wanted: 'I want them to be able to give you advice, to be knowledgeable but not too orderly, and to be quick. They often don't seem very interested in what they

173

are doing or know much about what they're selling unless they're the manager.' The kids were looking for information and advice. Partly because their money was precious and they didn't want to waste it but also because they were novices and wanted help in choosing the right product:

'They ought to tell you things, whether it crumples with wear, whether it's the right thing for my hair or can you use it on all different types of hair – obvious things like that because they're important.'

'I hate it when they say it looks great and it doesn't because you can't make up your mind yourself ... and if they haven't got what you want I'd rather they'd say then "We'll get some in later, so come back." '

'When you're young they just watch you and then they ignore you and you could be standing in the queue for ages and they serve everybody else but not you.' It's not surprising really that Harry gets fed up and pockets the item and walks out without paying.

The disdain many shop assistants held for the young was related to me by Jane and her friends:

'I wanted some new shoes, so she got me one off a display counter. So I said to her, "They're different colours," and she said, "Sorry, it's all we've got, take them or leave them." So I had to leave those ... then I went to get some sandals and all the inside soles started coming up so I had to take them back. The woman just started shouting at me, "I should have thought you could have found something to stick it down with at home." Then my mum took them back next day and they did it straight away, without a word, while she waited. If you take something back because you have to change it and you've worn it, you've only tried it on and it doesn't look right, they always think you have worn it, they look for crease marks and things like that.'

Harry had found the same attitude: 'I took a record back, it was faulty and the man was really heavy and said there was nothing wrong with it and I was having him on, but I managed to get my money back in the end.' What the adults don't understand is that those purchases are dear to the young. They've saved up for them and they feel really disappointed if they are faulty, and it can often mean paying extra money on bus fares into town too. The shop assistants never treat Mum like that. The young are also unsure or ignorant of their rights as consumers – that's another thing school doesn't teach them. But anyway they'd probably be much too shy and embarrassed to stand up to a stroppy assistant in a crowded store. They're not that confident yet.

Michelle was the lively ring leader who smoked dope, slept with her boy-friend, organized a school strike and argued continually with her mum. But underneath it all there was still the same adolescent shyness – she wasn't quite as grown up as she appeared:

'Up at Beach, there was this bloke I fancied and I wanted to buy some jeans. I couldn't get any to fit and I had to keep calling out "No, these don't fit," and I was getting very embarrassed, and I was writing out a cheque and my hand was shaking as I wrote it – oh I couldn't face that again.'

Carol and Mary had faced similar problems: 'I had to go into the chemist's to buy Tampax and there was this man in there and I had to go there because it was the only one open and I was so embarrassed ... Some men make you feel worse too, they ask you awkward questions and you go red and then they say, "Oh, you've gone red," and you feel even worse.'

Facing shop assistants was generally a nerveracking ordeal: 'I used to go bright red even when somebody asked me what size shoe I took.' 'I'm really nervous, I don't know what to say and I get tensed up and in a panic. I did some shopping once and then found I'd forgotten my money. Oh, it was awful.' Then there could still be Mum to face: 'Then after all that, it's been the wrong thing and Mum's made me take it back again.' An ordeal it could be, but when bravado was involved Michelle managed to lose her shyness: 'My sister wanted me to buy a suspender belt and there were all blokes around so I went into the shop with her, she had her back to the bloke in the shop and she was looking through all the drawers, making sure he couldn't see and she's picking them out looking at them. So I grabbed one and said, "Is this all right?" in a loud voice and she went "Ssshhh" and whispered yes ... so I just took it, slammed it down on the counter and said "How much?" She went bright red and walked out of the shop without me – and she's seventeen!'

Simon simplified everything though, he preferred Scouts to shopping: 'I like the catalogue, things in it are cheap, it's handy, they always have them in stock and there's no messing about in shops.'

Advertising

What role does advertising play in making the teenager into a consumer? They watch a lot of television, so are therefore very aware of TV commercials. They enjoy the ads that use humour, gimmicks or good music for their appeal and they had a universal hatred for the washing powder, margarine and tooth paste commercials – all advertising which is aimed at Mum and not them:

'I hate those new Bold 2 tests, they're always exaggerated. They say, "Can you tell which is cleaner?" but they probably use a new shirt and they've paid the lady to say it.'

'I hate those toothpaste ones, they always make out the one they are advertising is special and all the others are classed as ordinary, then next week there's another one on saying the same thing.'

Andy was cynical and wasn't going to get 'conned' into buying something just because the advertising used a super hero: 'You see ones with Kevin Keegan eating beef crisps, but I don't think anyone's going to go out and buy 'cause Kevin Keegan eats crisps so I'll go out and eat them as well.' Debbie at fourteen was a bit mixed up between the fantasy and reality in some advertising but she didn't take any notice because the situation they used was far outside her personal experiences: 'She puts this perfume on and this gorgeous looking man comes galloping up on a white horse just as soon as she puts the perfume on, that daft ... it could never happen ... I mean you wouldn't stand at the window like that would you? You'd shut the curtains.'

The advertising that did have an effect upon them was for

the products they would use or buy, such as food, drink, sweets, spot creams, cosmetics, sports wear:

'You see an advert for Walls Cornetto and you think, "I fancy that."'

'I bought Clearasil because I saw it advertised, but it didn't work.'

'Mary Quant adverts are really good ... they're really unusual ... they catch your eye ... they've got some really good eyeshadows.'

But sometimes the advertising had a different effect from the one required by the manufacturers. Beverly and Louise were discussing a commercial for baby products: 'That's a good one ... I want a little baby like that, not my own yet but ... I do too, I'm on at my mum to have another one ... that must be a good advertisement then!'

Overall, though, the young appreciated that advertising has a role to perform in telling consumers what products are available to buy, what they can spend their money on:

'It tells you what's in the shops, gives you ideas of how to spend money.'

'You try new things because you see them on telly or in magazines, and then you go along to Boots and smell it or look at it to see what you think ... if you don't like it you don't buy it.'

'There's lots of new products coming in the market all the time, they have to advertise them, if they put them straight in the shops no one would buy them.'

In the eyes of the young, television commercials seemed to add credibility and confidence to a product:

'I should think it would be quite good because they advertise it on telly.'

'I'd be more likely to buy something that I had seen advertised, because then you'd be sure it would work.'

'If they advertise something on telly it must be good, it shows they've got confidence in it.'

No matter how exciting the advertising or how attractive the shop window display, when considering the teenage consumer everything reverts to money. If they don't have the money, or their pocket money is reserved for other items then they can't buy it. 'You look around, see what's out and how much it all costs, and if you like it you can always go back later on when you've got the money.'

Saving

Whatever the role of advertising and window shopping there are levels of affluence that are vital to the kids for giving status amongst their friends, and worth struggling for. When Andy is out with the gang he must be able to buy chips and shandy with the rest of them, or his independence is only half-baked. Forbidden fruits are the most exciting. Mark is free to play the slot machines, try for an X-movie at £2.50 a go, buy fags, bubble gum and a packet of johnnies and take a train to Southend. Michelle can buy a low-cut glitter sweater, lipstick, and purple hair dye, fund a Pernod and blackcurrant in the pub and pay the cover charge at the Club Focus.

Harry's friend Andrew collects belt buckles and that's where his money goes: 'You get them from junk shops, second-hand shops, the leather shop and from catalogues and that. Now this shop's opened, I'm starting to save up a bit more and I'll be able to go down there once a month. They're going to start making holsters and bullwhips – that's what I'm saving my money for now. One person at school collects coins and one person collects engines, boat engines, lawn-mower engines ...' Even his girl-friend paled in comparison: 'That was the problem with Jackie – money. When I packed her in, I had enough money for buckles and records and that.'

Andrew is prepared to save up to get a really special belt buckle just as Michelle will save for a special dress and Simon will save for a special pair of trainers. Saving £1 a week makes a big hole in your income when you only get £2.50, but sometimes it is the only route to what you want. You can be sure that Simon really wants those trainers or he would never accept the discipline of saving for them. The teenagers we talked to weren't over-excited about wrist-watches, cameras, clock radios, hairdryers and the other mechanical paraphernalia which adults choose for status symbols. The nearest thing would be a racing bike, a Hi-fi or your own television set.

When you look at the endless list of teenage needs, it is astounding how much the kids actually do save. Two in every five are saving without any particular goal. Imagine, with all those pressures to consume, two out of five are saving because they think it's a good thing to save.

This is all thanks to Mum. Harry: 'During school weeks I get £10.50. My mum puts it away for me. Otherwise I'd only spend it.'

Ian: 'My mum takes half my money sometimes for holidays, to save it for me.'

There are all sorts of handy rationalizations for saving, like 'I want to have something by me, in case I see something,' or 'I'm saving for when I get married,' and even Sarah at twelve is establishing a relationship with the building society so that she can get a mortgage later on.

The real reason is deeper. Teenagers are afraid of running out of control. The child half of them is luring them on to blow the lot; like Sarah: 'Sometimes I wish I could just shove all my money in a bag and spend it,' and Kevin: 'This £5 that I've got now, I'm going to spend it tomorrow night, I'm going to get pissed tomorrow night.' But they won't get the things they *really* want unless they listen to the grown-up half. Joanne: 'I try to put it away, otherwise I will only spend it on other things which I don't really need.'

They are afraid of spending all their money, just as they are afraid of getting caught in a football riot, drinking too much or losing their temper. This is what Sarah is saying in her own way: 'Sometimes I don't spend my money, sometimes I spend a lot. If I'm feeling cross I spend all of it, I don't care what I do. I'm cross at everybody.' When I ask her why, I get no reply. Being cross and spending money are both ways to get back at adults.

Even though their wants are endless, four out of five kids think the money they get is fair. Like Harry, they don't want to be taken beyond the limits of their own control: 'You only need a little bit of money, you don't need a lot,' he says. 'You only need as much as you need.'

179

Ian at thirteen spells out the dilemma: 'It's hard to save, because there are so many things that you need all the time – sweets, LPs. You just forget to save. I wanted to go to a football match the other day, but I forgot all about it and spent all my money. There's a good thing that my mum does. She doesn't give me pocket money because I know I'd go out and spend it, and that'd be a waste. So what she does, if I want to go to the pictures, she gives me the money. But she wouldn't let me waste it. So when I want something I just ask her. But there's a limit to it.'

At every age some kids find it easy to save and others find it impossible, but all of them believe that they *ought* to save. Mum instills saving as a virtue and Joanne upholds it, though good sense says otherwise: 'If you save £200, in a couple of years inflation may have risen that much, and your money would hardly be worth anything.'

Me: 'Would it worry you or would you go on saving?'

Joanne: 'I'd go on saving.'

At twelve Sarah and Simon listen to Mum, and put away 50p a week. Simon is resigned: 'I think at first, there'll be a lot you want to spend your money on. Then you'll think and you'll stop and just save up.' The snooker table he has his eye on at £120 will take him two years to save up for at this rate. Sarah is saving for a horse, which costs £600, and a house for when she's older. In the meantime Mum gives her the odd 10p, and if she's lucky adds the cost of *Jackie* to the family paper bill.

It is not as simple for the boys. Ian, Andy and Harry *need* the cash day to day: 'I was a better saver when I was younger than I am now. I don't get enough to save,' mourns Harry. 'Definitely a spender,' confesses Andy. 'I used to be a saver but I'm a spender now!' Andy dreams of owning a motor bike, but it's so far out of his price range, that he may as well wait until he starts work before he starts saving in earnest. He gets better value for money by enjoying his £4.10 now, while a bag of chips is still a luxury and a record album is a passport to a cult of believers.

Girls are better at saving than boys are. They have to be, because most of their money goes on clothes. It takes well over a month to save up for anything worth having. The other big reason for saving is to have enough money for the family holiday: 'You need a lot of money for places like Ibiza,' says Joanne, who get's £2.50 a week, all in. 'So I would try to save about £40. I saved up to go to France last year and I paid for it myself.'

What could be better then, than going to Ibiza (or Ostend, or Blackpool) for a fortnight? The bars serve them Martini, the discos are humming with new people, and the girls are lifted out of themselves. Like dragonflies they fly for a day, so everything must be perfect – they must have new clothes and enough ready cash to grasp every opportunity: 'It takes a long time. Usually about seven months before we go, I will start to save up. But it's worth it.' Then, when she gets there Beverly lets rip: 'I can't help it, when I'm at a pleasure beach I just spend and spend and spend. When we went to Majorca we only went for a week. I must have spent a bomb, because the hotel is just a few doors away from the pleasure beach and I was there every day.'

Responsibilities

The talk so far has all been about kids spending money on themselves. The issues have either been 'What do I want money for?' 'How do I get more money' or 'How do I make sure I don't waste my money?' It takes a long time before the kids step back to consider spending their precious income on anyone else. Poor Beverly. 'I hate giving all my money out and not buying anything nice. I prefer to spend it on myself. I only buy something when it's birthday or Christmas.' But she feels obliged to buy presents for birthdays and Christmas, just as all the other girls do. Sometimes it seems as though the year is divided into two: 'I sort of save up from spring till the summer, then after the summer I start saving again until Christmas – for presents!' Presents take a big chunk out of her income: 'You can't get anything for under £1,' and she plans it well in advance. 'If I've got birthdays, or Mother's Day is coming up I cut down on what I'm spending, but there are always other things that you have to buy in between.'

The boys don't seem as conscience-stricken about it as the girls. The girls are more sensitive about Mum's money problems too. Fourteen-year-old Liz's mum is on Social Security, and much as Liz wants to go to the cinema with the gang, she won't ask her mum for extra because that isn't fair. Either she'll get it by baby sitting or she won't go. Beverly pumps Mum for an extra 20p every time she wants to go swimming or buy a bar of chocolate, but even she is struck by remorse:

'Prices are going up and up, and by the time my mum gets all her wages, she's paid for all the food for five and she's paid the rent and all this lot. By the time she's finished, she's only got about £5 to go out with. If she's spending it on me, you feel guilty because she never gets anything. It's always us getting things. My mum once took me out and she was buying loads of new things and she only bought things for me. So me and my sister, we saved up and we bought her a pair of shoes. She was very pleased because she wanted these shoes and she couldn't get them because she spent all the money on me. When we bought it for her, she wondered what it was. When she opened it, she was crying because she was happy.'

Eventually, the great day dawns when Mum's home-grown banking system has to yield to the chilling grandeur of a formal savings account. This is the parents' decision. Money is serious. For the first time, Dad is involved as well as Mum. You defer to their judgement, because they know more about it than you do, and you can't afford to make a mistake. Harry can argue with his dad until Domesday about the right way to tackle the new Maths, but he will open an account at Dad's bank without a murmur. Ian describes how he and his dad went to the bank together; 'I've had a bank account about one month. I was getting a lot of money from my paper round and keeping it in my bedroom. It was my dad's idea. He took me up on Thursday to the National Westminster. My dad's got an account there.' Half of Ian is proud of being admitted to Dad's world, his money is as good as any grown-up's! But the other half is defiant, it's too early to accept real financial responsibility. He liked it the old way: 'I don't get enough to save, why should I be interested?' Like Simon, Sarah and Beverly, Ian's blood-curdling view of banks sounds more like the Wild West than the High Street:

'If you have a bank robbery, all the money you've put in there, you've lost it and you have to start all over again. I'd rather be paid in cash, you'd know you weren't getting cheated then. You hear about these one-off banks that go bankrupted, then no one ever hears of their money again. Our bank's got a great big wooden door – hot, sticky, poky little place. I put my money there, then they put it in a tin box. Makes you feel small, you feel like a criminal, they all have bars.' Crouched like a black spider, in his back office web is the bank manager. It sounds like a torture chamber. 'Do you see your friendly bank manager with his axe? Has he got a hood on? Yes!'

Michelle swallows as she tells herself that the sinister manager is going to take over where Mum left off! 'Right, don't back out now. Just go in and ask one of the girls if I can see the manager, because I have an appointment. And remember, look pleasant and speak well.'

Harry isn't planning to hang around: 'They're all cross in the bank. They've all got special, bullet-proof windows. They've got these little cases, you put what you want in it. They pull it through, take it out, read what you want, shove it in, pass it back – and you're off!'

Sarah had a much better time with the building society. With gusto she acts out the ladylike way she was ushered in: 'This lady, when I went into the building society with £5, she said, "Good morning, let's see what you've got then." She was really nice. When I went in with my mum and dad, she took us in and we had a cup of coffee.'

At Sarah's age, girls on average have £68 saved up and the boys far outstrip them, with an average of £91. But the tables have turned at Michelle and Harry's age when, on average, the girls have £92 and the boys only £77.

Formal savings accounts aren't geared to the pace of teenage life. Banks are closed after school and on Saturdays, and they don't understand that as soon as Harry has saved £20 for a parka then he needs the money immediately to go out and buy it. They won't give him a cheque book until he's eighteen, so getting at his money isn't easy. 'For a bank, your parents can put in money,' he complains, 'but you have to be eighteen before you can get it out. In a building society you can get it whenever you want!'

Why do the kids bother with formal institutions at all? Well, for a start, they remove the money physically out of the way of temptation. 'I got an account there, so I could save it,' says Andy, 'so I couldn't get my hands on it and spend it.' But more important than all that, they give interest. 'You could get extra money added on.'

At twelve, Sarah doesn't know a lot about interest. She depends on Mum and Dad to make sure she's getting the best deal. But at fifteen, Andy spends his time comparing interest rates and congratulating himself on the extra money he has made. On his weekly budget *any* interest at all is money for jam: 'I got 26p interest on mine.' Eventually, he can get the money out and buy the new Angelic Upstarts' album. Suddenly he is reaping tangible rewards for saving. Bit by bit he tackles the system. Three out of every five teenagers believe that the building societies give the highest interest rate, but Andy has read the small print and knows that gross rates only apply to taxpayers. He's better off in the bank at 14 per cent until he's got a regular job. And he's ready to argue it out with the others:

Kevin: 'You get interest on it in the building society.'

Andy: 'Yes, but you're not gaining much on that are you?'

Gerald: 'You're not gaining anything.'

Kevin: 'You are – you're getting about 12 per cent – that's quite a lot.'

Andy: 'It's 12½ per cent in the post office – it's 15 per cent in the banks.'

Kevin (defeated): 'You're not really gaining or losing because all the prices are going up.'

Gerald: 'The worth of a pound is going down.'

Andy's keen to keep up his relationship with the building society, though, because one day he'll want to buy a house. It's difficult to get him to focus on the future, but this is one issue he's set on. 'I've got something in the building society

184

building up, it's to help you get a house. If you save with them long enough they give you a mortgage when it comes to the time to get a house. My sister's boy-friend he's got a chance to get the house they wanted.'

If you think of it in black and white terms loans are the opposite of saving, so if saving is a virtue, credit must be a vice. Two-thirds of teenagers fear they will get into debt too easily if they are allowed to use credit and are even more determined never to use hire purchase. Cheques are suspect because they revive the old worry that the money will run away with them. Kids from working-class families are a third more suspicious of cheque books than kids from 'white-collar' families, although even they fancy having a cheque book to flash around: 'It would be nice to have a cheque book in your bag,' admits Michelle. Michelle is not as wary of credit as she used to be and she can see the day when she will own a credit card as well as a cheque book. But her brother persists in dealing on a cash only basis. 'You can always trust cash, you can't always trust a cheque.' Mind you, credit cards are about as clear as mud to a teenager. 'You can spend a certain amount of money up to £50 on that card, explains Ian. They do it through your building society or whatever it is, and take it out of that. With the banks you can get cards. You can have cards sent to say that you have got so much money in. On building societies you can't, that's what I mean.'

One bit of plastic looks much like another, and kids under eighteen aren't allowed to have them anyway.

Mortgages are (literally) nearer home. Mortgages are an allowable form of debt and everybody expects to have one eventually. At thirteen Beverly has got the idea 'You pay so much a week. It's because if you took all the money to pay for your house all at once ... you put a mortgage to it and when you can, you put the mortgage back again. If you don't pay that money in a certain time you have to pay more than you have to.' But Sarah can't cope: 'It's when you put some money back for a house but you don't use it for yourself. I think it's a good thing, because if you have to pay back the money, you're saving it and not spending it on anything else.

But the people in the banks should have the money because you might spend it anyway. You're saving up and probably see something that's really expensive and you haven't got the right money, but you realize you've got the money for the mortgage, so you probably spend that and then you've got to start saving up again!'

Hard earned reality?

But one thing nobody can avoid is inflation, everybody has felt its effects and now it is the norm. A whole generation of kids like Beverly are growing up believing that inflation will go on for the rest of their lifetime: 'They're all going up the prices – and you're not going to afford things. My mum at one time she could get a basketful of shopping for about £5 and she gets only half that now for the same amount. You can imagine what prices will be when we're older.' She senses she is being exploited: 'It must be inflation with prices, you're paying for the price of that box, also the name, and you're paying for VAT as well. We are paying taxes and we are paying to publicize it.'

Andy also feels aggrieved. He's been done down by keeping his money in the bank: 'I got £10.70 interest. It was only about £20, but still I expected more. You think of inflation you know, for ten years and you had £20 in there and inflation going up about 40 per cent. It has gone up more than that, so you should get that interest. If inflation goes up 50 per cent next year, it's just not worth it.'

Joanne does economics at school and she believes the government does it on purpose; 'If people get a rise at work the government has to put up prices to pay for the rises.'

How can you win?

But they find it very hard to get interested enough to talk about it. The system is too abstract, they think in terms of what they can see. After sixteen, most of them will have said goodbye to formal education, and one wonders how much more sophisticated their understanding is going to get. Perhaps they will simply attach big words to the same oversimplified concepts. If teenagers don't really know how it all hangs together, when they enter the job market, who is going to take the trouble to teach them later on? Isn't it likely that they will cling to ideas which look right on the surface, without understanding their broader implications? Already Andy is saying that if inflation goes up 50 per cent, his bank balance should go up 50 per cent as well. If that happens, it won't be long before we see galloping price rises, instant poverty for people on fixed incomes, no foreign goods for sale, and a mad rush for gold.

For the kids, being able to manage your own money gives you independence from other people's rules. But there's not a lot of hope for the independent citizen if he can't understand enough about economics to know what's in his best interests. In reality, his options are being gobbled up by the politicians who make financial decisions on his behalf. Money governs politics these days. At least the kids should be helped towards an understanding of what they'll be voting for. Mum can't teach them enough and the banks don't try to. Shouldn't money management be a school subject equal to the three 'R's?

11 Future roles

Me: 'What's good about being you, your life now?'

'I've got a lot of friends, I like school, I go out quite a lot, I go to discos, the pictures every Sunday, it's quite fun.'

Andrew is fourteen, almost fifteen, and is happy with his life, he enjoys himself. But how long will it last? Into adulthood? That's all in the future for him, and the other boys and girls I talked to. How do they see the world that is in store for them? What's the world like through the eyes of an adolescent? How do they see us, grown-ups?

Getting a job

Their first step into adult society is leaving school and getting a job. Overall, they're very happy at school but just slightly under two-thirds of them said they were looking forward to getting a full-time job – that's not surprising as jobs provide the money they are so desperately short of.

'School's OK but you don't get no flaming money.'

Everyone wanted an interesting job that paid well: 'Not just like an office job, it would be so boring sitting there typing, it does get you a bit of money – but I'd get so bored. I don't want to wake up every morning thinking "Oh God, work again."'

Despite looking forward to a job, most of the sixteen-year-olds were just as vague as the eleven-year-olds about leaving school: 'I'll wait until the time comes and then think about it.'

'That's all they ever go on about at home – jobs, jobs, jobs, I can't think of anything now.'

'It's a bit early to think about a job ... I just don't want a job that's boring and where I'm doing the same thing all the time.'

Professional guidance was practically non-existent and

everyone went on luck or the experiences of someone they knew, usually family:

'It's all a matter of chance and if you get the right chances you'll take them.'

'My dad knows a man who said he might be able to get me into the diamond business.'

'Do what my dad does, there's good money in it.'

'My teacher says I'm good in languages so I'd like to be a skiing instructor.'

They had very little concrete idea of what to do. I was forcing them to talk about it and most of their choices involved a form of fantasy and were not based on the reality of needing qualifications or finding opportunities:

'A psychiatrist, they get paid well and if you go to America you can come back and earn a fortune.'

'I want to work with animals, if I can't be a vet I'll just work with them and not get paid.'

Me: 'But how will you live?'

'I don't know, I'll live with the animals if I have to.'

Me: 'But how will you keep a roof over your head?'

'I don't know.'

'My uncle was in the army and it sounds good, they have night exercises and camping and like in the advert they pretend they're really attacking a town or a major city.'

Michelle, however, had a sense of humour about it: 'I'm going to be in computers, because we are all going to be run by computers eventually, and if I can work out how to fiddle them, I'll have a lovely life!'

Because the boys and girls had no experience themselves of the world of work, they relied upon parents, relatives, teachers, television and the press to give them an insight.

But all these sources gave them a very narrow outlook and maybe that is why they thought in terms of very traditional jobs. When we talked generally the boys and girls said they believed in sexual equality and equal rights but when it came to thinking about jobs, they obviously had not got that far. Girls wanted to help people, to be secretaries, typists, nurses, hair dressers, beauticians, models, actresses, teachers, to work with children or animals, to be air hostesses etc:

'If I was an air hostess I could talk to all the passengers; if they were nervous I'd calm them down ... like they did in the film *Airport*.'

'Be a secretary and travel, my teacher said I'd be a good secretary, I'd type, take phone messages for my boss and I'd like to travel as well.'

'I love playing with my friends' hair and I do my mum's too ... you get something out of it when you've finished and it looks good.'

Boys on the other hand wanted to *do* things, to be mechanics, engineers, electricians, work with computers, go into the forces or the police, to be architects, drivers, footballers etc:

'Be a civil engineer, my uncle is, and is doing very well in America and I like to be outside, not in the office.'

'Play football for a big club and get 30,000 wanting you – to dream of going to Wembley and hear people shouting your name.'

The forces seemed popular and a way of avoiding growing up. The boys could continue playing games and having adventures, they were looked after and the discipline meant they didn't have to make any decisions – much like home and Mum really:

'I wanted to go in the RAF, I don't think about the defence side, the weapons, but I've always loved aircraft and wanted to fly. Planes have a lot of elegance and when you're a pilot and you get up there you can do what you want.'

'I've always been interested in planes! I get loads of books out of the library and memorize all the facts of every plane going. I'm always going to the airport, just to look at planes.'

'I'll probably go with one of the forces because there you don't have to get a job. My dad was on at me, he was in the army and he thinks it's good because it gives you self-discipline ... you get a lot of money and take orders.'

The idea of responsibility was daunting at this age: 'I wouldn't like to go straight in as an officer, they'll think you're a right snob, I'd rather work my way up.' Not all the boys were as enthusiastic about the forces and some were cynical:

The army is for failures, you don't need exams, it's for

people with nothing else to do, they're not looking for brains, just brawn.'

'The navy is full of poufs, like Village People.'

'If you go in the army you might get your head blown off.'

'If you went in the police force you'd lose all your mates, they'd all be against you.'

There were more examples of differences in attitudes between the boys and girls. When they were given a list and asked to tick off what they thought were the most important aspects of a job, boys were more concerned about high wages, promotion, a good training, challenges and long term security, whereas the girls were more interested in the less aggressive aspects such as personal satisfaction, working with people and being able to help people.

Girls' attitudes to work, though, are inconsistent with their aims at school. Slightly more girls than boys expect to get their O and A levels but half the girls expected to go to college or university compared with just over a third of boys. Something seems adrift between wanting to go to university and wanting to be a hairdresser or typist.

But the economic situation was having a real effect on some of the older boys who took notice of the news, especially those in the North, and they were beginning to appreciate the need for exams too:

'I think about it a lot now because its getting much nearer but I really don't know what to do ... the trouble is the prospects are getting worse, there's too many redundancies and strikes, there won't be any choice soon, you'll have to have lots of qualifications just to work in a factory.'

'It's a question of getting what job you can, not what you want, it makes you realize you must get your qualifications.'

The economic situation certainly seems to be introducing a serious note into the young. Andy is a bright vivacious fourteen-year-old Londoner, very involved in music and fashion, and he reflected a very up to date point of view: 'Jobs, there aren't any, it's depressing, gloomy, now when you hear the news they always have to save a good bit for the end ... I see a Porsche and I think I'd love one but when I think of what job I could do to get that, I don't know ...

there doesn't seem much chance I'll ever get one. It's all a bit scarey. In a way you are forced to think now because at school you have to choose options and you have to think of what O levels I should take in order to get a job in the future. I think further education is worth it if it combines your qualifications and gets a better job and gives you more choice.'

But the thought of actually going to work was still unreal for many kids, they had no idea what it was like:

'I'll just sit in an office with a cup of tea earning £200 a week, I'll just sit there drawing little squiggles.'

'I can't make up my mind whether to be a plumber or a banker. A man came round last week to unblock our bath and it looked quite interesting.'

Setting up a home
The world of work is largely unknown to the young, but how do they see those links they do have with adult society, those they are close to such as Mum, Dad, grown-ups, how do they think of the family and marriage?

Marriage was obviously important, it would give them a stable background, and it was always present when the girls were talking together, they took it for granted they would get married and have children. Boys, however, only mentioned it when I asked them about it. But they weren't that different from the girls, they knew it was inevitable and accepted it. None of them wanted to get married *now*, it was in the future, and they also saw it as the end of their fun. Tina and her friends said: 'Wouldn't it be funny if one of us got married at sixteen, just imagine we'd have to say "Oh, I've got to go home now," and feel left out of it because everybody else would be living it up and doing whatever they wanted ... and you'd be married.'

Marriage was popular, only 3 out of a 100 didn't want to get married and they expected to be married by the time they were 23. It was the girls who saw marriage as actually affecting their life style and they wanted to achieve something before they had their children. 'I won't get married for a long time yet, I'll be at least eighteen or twenty, I want to make a go of my life first, try and get O and A levels. I won't get married until I've got my A levels then when I have a kid I can get a good job with money.' They expected to have children by the time they reached twenty-five.

'Everyone's got that feeling that they'd like having a baby, watching it grow up.'

'I want to be a young Mum so I can understand my kids when they're my age, you can't communicate with someone who's so much older.'

'I want to have children, but not until I've lived most of my life ... twenty-five, no earlier.'

Tina wasn't that happy at home, she wanted to get married and settle down: 'It's security, if you don't settle down then you're spending all your time getting to know people and that. If you do settle down you haven't got any problems any more and you just get to know each other.' Her friend just wasn't ready for settling down though: 'I'd get bored, I'm sure, and you never know if they'll get bored and walk off.'

Simon was living in the suburbs of Manchester and he had a very traditional, serious outlook on life. He didn't necessarily reflect all boys' views about marriage but he was one of the few to talk about it in any depth: 'You want to feel you're in charge of something, people like pop singers don't have wives and then they take drugs and all that, they have no one to control or stop them ... look at Elvis Presley, what happened to him. In marriage you've got someone to care for, possess something, you're settled.'

Ian wasn't so sure though — it was nice to be settled but he still wanted his freedom too: 'I think I want to be by myself really, to do what I want. When you've got a wife she'll nag you and want to watch opera all the time ... and it means you get someone talking at you all the time.'

When they did get married most of the young people expected to live where they were living now, they didn't see themselves moving away. Tina, being a Londoner, certainly didn't want to move far: 'No, I'm not going to the suburbs, all the houses look the same, I can picture it now, all the husbands leave at the same time, for the same sort of jobs, and the wives sit there all day and do their housework and pat the dog on the head.'

Remote their view of marriage might be, but the girls didn't seem prepared to model themselves on Mum. They loved Mum and didn't want to leave her, but when I pushed one group of girls into telling me how they saw their Mum they were far from romantic, maybe this is what the generation gap is all about:

'I want to be interesting, my mum's boring.'

'My mum works too hard, she does about four jobs, she's always working hard and she doesn't ever get a lot of money.'

'My mum's always in a bad mood, always depressed.'

'My mum's OK but she doesn't do anything all day, she just slops around.'

'My mum's always having a go at me about something.'

The girls seemed to resent the inevitable routine:

'I've seen what they're doing and I've seen what it has made them into and I think ... Oh God ... get up in the morning, go to work, come home, switch on the telly, have a meal and go to bed again.'

'She comes home from work, goes out in the evening to a pub, gets pissed and that's it – home again.'

What these teenagers hated was that their mums didn't seem to 'do anything' – although they had no idea how they would be different.

Dads weren't talked about much, they were not at home as much as Mum so there were less chances to talk to each other. But everyone hated, and wanted to avoid, family rows and arguments. When the boys and girls interviewed were asked to complete the sentence, 'I am most miserable when ...' roughly one in five said when there were rows at home – the young wanted a secure, stable home. It was a bit like teachers and school, they liked to know where they stood: 'My parents care for me and want me to be happy in life, but they should be more open-minded. But I do hate those parents who let their kids do anything and don't even mind if they get in trouble with the police.'

They know they're going to leave home, probably before

they get married. The prospect of leaving became more exciting as they grew older but also a bit scarey too because it was nice to have Mum to look after them. But as time passed the yearning for freedom from rules and regulations increased, especially in the girls: 'There's always pressure at home, you're somebody's responsibility; when you leave home you're freer, you need your parents but you don't want them all the time.'

'At home you have to come in when they say, not be out in the dark, have to rely on them all the time ... I'm looking forward to getting a job where I bring home my *own* money and to be able to afford a tiny flat ... but I'll need a good job to pay the rent.'

'It's exciting leaving home ... you want to know what life is all about even if you know it's going to be horrible ... it will be quite hard always needing money for the rent ...'

Me: 'But what about paying the bills, buying your own food?'

'That's something I look forward to ... I just can't wait to get out there and try it on my own.'

Me: 'Suppose it doesn't work out, you can't do it?'

'Easy, I come back home.'

For most though, this step was much more into the future, now they were too shy and lacking in confidence. Debbie led a sheltered life in Sheffield and was not looking forward to work: 'I'm scared I'm not ready for it. I don't think I could cope with things. I won't know where to start, what to do ... My mum will have to tell me and help me.' Her friend was the same: 'I want to be older when I leave school, I've not got a lot of confidence. I'll want to be more sure of myself or I'll feel everyone is closing in on me.'

Up against adults, not only their parents, they saw themselves as being forced into the silent minority, and that was exasperating:

'When they talk to you as a child you have to listen to them, but then they don't listen to *you*, you always have to respect your elders, they always have to be right.'

'You always have to be silent when adults are around, but then they butt into your conversations and they have power over you if you answer back, like teachers who can give you bad marks.'

'At bus stops they think they own the buses, and if you're just in the queue they try and get over you and when you're first in a shop queue they budge in front just because they're older.'

'Grown-ups are called tarts but it's not the same because adults do more than what children do, they go further; but a girl only has to kiss a few boys and she's a tart.'

All so unfair.

Too young to vote
The adults they really didn't understand or have any time for were the politicians. Margaret Thatcher came in for lots of criticism from the young of all ages and was very unpopular, largely due to education policies and rising prices:

'What about the education cuts, I really hate her, she's only trying to help the rich get richer and education cuts make no difference to them, they all send their kids to private schools.'

'The rich get richer and the poor get poorer. I've seen my family get worse since she's been there.'

'She said there wouldn't be any strikes.'

'The Conservatives have caused total chaos and Margaret Thatcher's told lies.'

'She makes me sick, she wants us to go to school on Saturday morning, that means you can't work and suppose you go to a party. You don't expect to have to go to school next day.'

'She gets everything wrong – a nosey old bag that's all I can say ... she makes things go up and yet everybody went for her because she said they are going to come down ... last year our crisps were 7p, she came in and they were at 8p and now they're 9p and school dinners have gone from 25p to 55p too.'

'She's doing a good job ... oh yea ... so good we've not got enough paper to write on at school .. she's turning into a dictator'

'She's for the rich, she should help people who aren't rich, who can't look after themselves.'

'It's bad when they cut back education and school, I don't like Margaret Thatcher, school dinners and loads of sweets have gone up in price.'

The young took politics very much on face value and everything was black or white. But anyway, who cares about politics? 'It's just boring for us, they're always talking, and *we* can't change anything so what's the point?'

'It's nothing to do with us. I'm too young to vote so I don't bother, anyway people just ignore us and what we have to say, they don't care what we think about politics so why should we worry ... it doesn't matter what party's in really ... it's all one big con.'

Simon spoke for most of the young people, they all felt apart from it and saw little difference between the parties: 'It's all so daft, the Conservatives come in now, they say they have all the mess to clear up that Labour left and if you got rid of the Conservatives then Labour are going to have to clear up that again before they make a move ... they ought to have just one party, some from every side all joined in together. Labour and Conservatives just disagree for the sake of an argument.'

The kids didn't seem to be in favour of any of the parties particularly. When asked what they thought about voting Labour a third were favourable, a third against and a third simply didn't know.

In many ways adolescents are still very young and because they don't understand politics, they take the arguing as 'real' equivalent to rows at home, particularly when associated with international politics: 'They're always arguing and criticizing each other, but it causes wars and I worry about it, things like Iran and Afghanistan. I don't know what its all about, they might end up blowing up the world.' 'Politicians are always fighting and arguing, they're always going to do something but never do – I don't know why they argue.'

Tina did learn about politics at school: 'Trouble is it's so hard to grasp things like strikes ... I forget why they go on strike, it's all so complex politics,' but Simon didn't. I asked him what he thought bureaucracy meant. 'I don't know what it means ... I've never heard of it ... is it anything to do with justice?' It all comes back to the fact that kids at school somehow remain untouched by it all, unaffected and uninterested: 'It's all getting worse but it won't affect us for years.' 'It just doesn't affect you, not people of our age, inflation doesn't affect me, I've never been used to anything cheaper, if inflation goes up so does our pocket money.'

But patriotism is not dead and the Queen was popular, 73 per cent agreeing that she should be there. They may be keen to travel but Britain was best:

'I'm British to the core ... we've got our Queen ... we can say what we like ... we may not have that much money but we're better off in our life ... more freedom.'

'We've got the countryside and stuff like that.'

'I'm used to it, I don't want to leave it ... there's always a lot of different things going on ... it's always lively ...'

But there were reservations: 'If you've got the money, you've always got Income Tax to think of ... violence is getting worse and the Mods and Rockers are fighting in town.'

Them and us and snobs

Politics may mean nothing to the young but class does. They put forward the strong belief that we are still living in a class-dominated society. Yet again, in their eyes all aspects of life are simplified into basics. For the young there are 'them' and 'us', rich and poor, upper-class and working-class, plus 'snobs'.

The upper classes were always rich, and they were easy to sort out because they were so different from you, your family and friends:

'They stay younger longer, they never seem to dress up or anything but they look smart. They don't wear older clothes so they tend to stay young, although they spend a lot of money on their clothes they don't look as if they do because it looks different ... they spend a lot of money on things like horses too.'

'They have big houses, live in London and send their children to private schools and their sons inherit it all.'

'Have two cars, a dishwasher and someone to clean the house.'

They are also seen to have Margaret Thatcher on their side, and anyway politicians were part of that group of our society.

'Snobs' were a group apart. At their own age they were the ones who didn't join in, didn't follow fashion, always did their homework, talked differently. 'She's a snob, she's got everything she wants and she says Mummy and not Mum.' 'They don't mix in with the other kids and have parties all the time.' But what they hated most about snobs was: 'It's the way they look down on you.' 'They act as if you're not good enough for them.' 'It's not money, it's the way they act and the way they look down on people.'

These young people were unsure what social class they were. We know we were talking to a range of classes because we had their forms filled in with their fathers' occupations, but as far as they were concerned they were 'us', which broadly meant the working classes. It was difficult for the kids to talk about class, because when they did they were usually dealing with stereotypes, often based on famous people they saw in the press and on television. In their narrow world of home and school everybody was divided into 'them and us', they had not had the opportunity to meet people for whom other categories were needed, may be that would come when they left school and started work. Beverly's comments show the confusion:

'It annoys me. We're not particularly poor really, or rich, but now we've got a car and we go on holiday abroad, but you walk past some people's houses and there is all sorts of cars outside and they're always going abroad.'

They held equal disdain though for the other extreme: 'Why should the scroungers be allowed, those who refuse to work and live on the dole?' There was a hint though of deeper, bitter, feelings about 'them' and this came out in a discussion with Andy, a fifteen-year-old Londoner, about the potential third World War:

'They will have caused it and we will have to suffer, but this time we won't fight and everyone will go round and smash up rich people's houses ... next time there won't be any of this "good luck old chaps" that you see in old war films, now it's all different.'

Tina lived on a large council estate and didn't feel so bitter, just resigned: 'We won't get a chance to get rich, we won't get the opportunities. You can't get rich just by working hard and in lots of the jobs that could make you rich, you need money to get into anyway ...'

Although they separated the rich from people like 'us', they were not particularly anxious to be wealthy themselves. A third of them certainly worried about not having enough money, but that was on par with teenage spots and not as much of a worry as school, exams, unfairness or getting a job.

Likewise, when asked to complete the sentence 'I would most like to ...' material possessions and wealth came second to 'travel', and only a quarter completed the sentence 'I wish that ...' with any reference to money.

Where class differences did become obvious was in the educational expectations of the young. Twice as many young people from the middle classes expected to pass A levels than did those from working classes, and twice as many working-class kids expected to leave school at sixteen, than did middle-class kids.

Black and white

Race didn't concern most young people. More than eight out of ten agreed with a statement that 'Black people are as good as white'; 'I've got nothing against black people, they're only different colours and a different accent ... a boy in our class gets the odd banana boy joke every now and then but then he calls us Honkeys and we joke about everyone.' Michelle's school had a high proportion of coloured kids; 'People in our school haven't got anything against coloured people. I haven't, I get on really well with them and I hate it when teachers are unfair to them ... I just don't want to mix with racist people.' Even the Skinheads weren't as racist as they appear to adults and examples were given of Skins who had black friends, even a black Dad, yet supported the National

Front because it was a symbol of the cult. So although on the one hand they are more liberal than past generations, it is not quite that simple. Many of the children we talked to come from areas where there are few coloured people so they rarely come into contact with them. Also, when you quiz the young more closely there is some prejudice against Asians: 'West Indians are OK but Pakis bug me, they think they're it.' But the reason for this is not their colour, it's because they act like 'snobs', not mixing in, keeping themselves apart and so the resentment builds up:

'I had some trouble with one of them once and now I've got it fixed in my head that they're all the same. They keep themselves to themselves and don't like mixing with white people and if you walk past them then they always make comments about you and everything.'

Me: 'But don't white people do that too?'

'No, that's different, that's a joke and you take it as a joke...'

'It takes so long to get to know them, they look down on you, they're snobbish, they try and buy you with crisps and sweets and money.'

'They go round in a gang all on their own.'

West Indians were accepted more readily as 'one of us' because they wore the same clothes, spoke the same language and usually knew where to score some dope:

'West Indians get on with you, they're good at sport and muck in with you, but the Pakis don't get on as well, they wear turbans, but the West Indians don't go round with spears in their hands and they wear what we wear. The Pakis always look so weak and feeble too, and the girls are quiet.' So it wasn't colour prejudice, just resentment of anyone who wasn't like them. Music is an essential element of the whole youth scene and Harry came up with the main problem. 'You never see any Paki groups in the Top Twenty. You see coloured stuff, reggae and Two Tone but where are the Pakis?'

In world terms, however, the young do seem to be chauvinist: 'In the Western world there's always plenty of everything, you take it for granted ... when you hear these appeals for money for Cambodia and things like that I think it would be better spent on cancer research or kidney machines. We should sort out our problems before anyone else's ... look after our own kind first.'

Equal rights

What about today's boys and girls who have been brought up with the Equal Pay Act and the Equal Opportunities Commission to think about sexual equality? Overall, there was an acceptance that men and women should have the same opportunities and receive equal pay: 'Of course women should have a choice ... a woman should be allowed to do what she wants if she's got the qualifications.' 'I agree with parts of equal rights for women but not all, and women do have the right to their own career.'

Two-thirds of the kids we interviewed agreed that men and women should be paid the same, but aggressive women worried both boys and girl. They were unsure of 'extremist women'. Only one third agreed that women should fight hard to be equal with men:

'Trouble is it's a bit like race, it can cause trouble if they're forcefully trying to get jobs ... When I get married I expect my wife to be equal in everything but I don't like dominant wives'.

'I don't like women who go to extremes and fight to be miners.'

Equality in the home was accepted and they believed men should help out with the housework:

'I used to think men looked after the money and all that but times are changing ... they swap more, men do the cooking and washing up and look after the children too ... perhaps in the past they've left women with too much.'

'One morning I'll get up at five and feed the baby and the next morning he'll do it.'

But there was still some resistance and a third firmly believed that a woman's place is in the home. When the girls discussed working they nearly always made the reservation about it having to fit in with a marriage and children:

'It's difficult working when you're married because of the young children. I'd have to find part-time work.'

'I want to be an air hostess but you can't when you have children.'

All these attitudes, however, are to do with marriage and the future. Apart from this theoretical agreement with equal rights and opportunities, equality was hardly discussed at all. Boys accepted girls and girls seemed to take their future for granted without thinking their sex would hold them back, but there was a definite feeling of difference between the sexes. Nor is it surprising, since they are at the stage of sorting out what manhood and femininity are all about. Younger girls of eleven and twelve, however, seemed much more aggressive about entering the male world. Simon felt threatened by them: 'There's a girls' football team at our school and they're quite good but now they're trying to get on the rugby pitch too ... that's terrible, we'll never get away from them, nothing's sacred – they're quite big some of those first years, suppose they beat us!'

At other times girls liked to hide behind their sex: 'It's all right for girls, you don't have to fight, only if you're poor or dress like a Mod or if nobody likes you.' 'The boys have to prove they're a man now, like the Skinheads.' Girls hated the fact that boys got much more personal freedom, could stay out later at night and had no worry about getting pregnant. 'I want a boy if I have one because they're less trouble and don't get pregnant and all they have to do is ask a girl to marry them.'

Inequality was there too when it came down to how you looked. Girls dressed up and tried to look nice for boys but accepted that a handsome boy could get away with looks alone. At home boys still tended to have their way over what programmes were watched on TV, and Mum was likely to insist that daughters helped with the washing up. There are signs of change though, with boys now just as likely as girls to cook at home and when going out and dating boys and girls tend to go 'dutch' and pay for themselves at the pictures or disco. Mixed schools appear to have had the most effect in increasing the communication between the sexes. In Tina's gang at school there were equal numbers of boys and girls and they'd all sit and talk together in the playground – they took each other for granted.

Much more subtle differences between boys and girls became clear however, when we looked at some of their answers to the questionnaire. When they were asked to describe themselves, boys and girls equally saw themselves as bored, lazy, lonely, having lots of friends, interested in lots of different things etc. But when it came to describing their level of self-confidence boys were twice as likely to describe themselves as good looking, and were more inclined to see themselves as clever than were the girls. Girls also emerged as more influenced by friends and generally more nervous than the boys. So boys are more self-confident and girls more inclined to self-doubt at this age.

When it came to educational goals the girls had higher expectations than the boys, but what happens when they think about jobs? They show a low level of ambition by going for the traditional female jobs. This further accentuates their lack of self-confidence, yet also provides some conflict with their desire to be different from their mum and her generation.

The future – doom and gloom?
How do they see the future – bearing in mind they find it hard to think more than two weeks ahead, or at least any further than the next party or disco date?

What looms large in the minds of adolescents of all ages is world peace and a likely third World War. More than four out of ten kids were concerned about what the world will be like when they are older, and when asked to say what they wanted in life, one in ten said world peace. But one of the frustrations of the young is their helplessness and inability to have any effect on society – they are too young to vote, and they see politicians starting the conflicts:

'The Ayatollah will get out of bed on the wrong side and it will all be over.'

'I worry that the Russians will drop a nuclear weapon and Britain will sink, you have to care about that.'

'Politicians start it all, the people don't know what's going on, it's the politicians that fight over the table, they do it for themselves they don't care about us.'

'The world is in a state, it's all a bit of a mess, everyone knows there'll be a third World War if the politicians get on with it the way they are now and they will have caused it and we just have to suffer, but this time no one will fight.'

The economic situation was expected to get worse in the future and it concerned many of the older boys and girls. The main way they saw it affecting them was in terms of job prospects. Roughly three-quarters of the boys and girls said they were really worried about getting a job when they left school and they were beginning to appreciate the need to pass their exams. Tina and Michelle both lived in London where there were more opportunities than for Harry who lived in Leeds, or Chris in Newcastle, but Tina was concerned and she had at least another year to think about it:

Me: 'What does the economic situation mean to you?'

'It's going to be harder for us to get a job ... I'll probably stay on at school if it's going to be hard to get a job at a later stage, it means you've got to get a lot of exams as a lot of kids will have a lot ... but there's not going to be much chance of getting jobs.'

Me: 'What will you do?'

'Don't know, I might have to sign on, there'll be restrictions on what we can buy, we won't have any money – I suppose that means we're in a depression ... Most people try not to think about it, it's depressing ... parents are always giving me lectures about school these days, how you must get all your O and A levels.'

Harry was less reflective. 'The Conservatives are spoiling my chance of a job ... all the trouble they've caused, it's total chaos.'

It sounds like propaganda from the school staff but school kids did wonder about the sense of education cuts. 'They're cutting money on schools and it's our generation who are going to run the country so they should be making it better not worse,' but they were not that surprised because they consider politicians as so far removed.' 'We've got all these old MPs of sixty, they don't know what we want or should have and they don't particularly care either ... but they wouldn't know as they're rich and all their kids go to private schools.'

Although quite a number of the kids wanted to work with computers and the new technology, fifteen-year-old Andy showed some concern that it might cause unemployment: 'By the time we're old enough everything will be done by computers and there'll only be hard labouring jobs left – or to go on the dole ... our teacher told us we really ought to be worried and he felt sorry for us, but most kids went home and thought nothing of it ... but that's rubbish, there'll always be jobs for men, look at the police, robots can't take their place and someone's got to make *them*.'

The state of street violence in the future concerned some of the London kids. Andy worried about safety because as a boy he was more likely to get involved himself:

'You can't go out like you used to, there are security guards everywhere, you worry about being attacked, you're always cautious about yourself. Every time a kid comes up to you in the street your heart stops and you get yourself prepared ... safety in the streets is important.'

'They pick you out just because you might wear something different or you might be poor, anything, and if you can't cope with it you have to be able to fight.' Tina described the gangs and fights that happened between the various council states in her area, where you'd get picked on just because of where you lived. I asked her whether this type of violence worried her, and what about the future, but she seemed to be part of a new breed of young women: 'It's all stupid really, we don't consider it all that bad, we've got used to it now ... anyway, we've learnt to take care of ourselves. At school we do judo, football things like that and as it's a mixed school, we know how to stand up for each other and ourselves.'

But it was difficult to think about the future. 'It's hard because we don't know what's going to happen from one day to the next so we might as well live it as it comes ... we normally end up sitting in someone's house totally bored ... we'll just come out with something, have a conversation about it, like how we're going to be, wondering if we'll know each other in the future ... lots of conversations about the world ending in five years' time ... that would be good.'

Me: 'What would you do if it was going to end?'

'Walk into a shop and take everything I wanted, have a last fling and shoot everyone I hated ... all of them, ding, ding, ding ... boys you liked and didn't know if they liked you, you could ask them out ... after all who's going to care if you've only got five years anyway?'

When asked what this country would be like in twenty years' time, 56 per cent thought it would be worse than it is now.

Real worries

Leaving aside the problems of the society they lived in, what were they worried about and what did they want out of life?

The agile mind of a teenager can switch in and out of subjects without pausing. We were talking about violence and the fear of being accosted in the street, and I asked what really worried them. 'Spots, as soon as I've got a spot coming, out comes the cream.' They worried a lot about their appearance, it was vitally important to the young. After all, that was how they were judged by the gang. So spots, appearance, not having the clothes I want, and not having my hair the way I want it were real worries.

Girls will always worry about boys it seems. 'Boys, everything you do is for boys, you don't want spots for boys, you want to look nice for boys and you take more care over yourself when there's a boy you fancy ... all boys are interested in is what a girl looks like.' But boys showed much less concern about girls. Boredom and finding things to do was a continual problem especially in the holidays. An extreme solution, but that was why Tina turned to glue sniffing. A quarter of the boys and girls were worried about not having enough to do in the evenings and at weekends and one in ten got particularly fed up when it was raining. 'I get bored ... I'm always trying to find something to do, trying to occupy your mind during the holidays.'

It didn't figure a lot in the discussions but came out in the questionnaires that unfairness and injustice was also a worry; one in two were upset by being told off for something they hadn't done and two in five about being picked on.

To stand out from the crowd

When asked about the things they wanted out of life there were differences between the answers that came back on the questionnaires and those given by the kids themselves and the differences was in the degree of emotion. From the questionnaire the kids wanted a variety of things — to travel, be healthy, leave school, be independent, succeed at school, sport, be happy and succeed in showbiz or the arts.

In discussion though, they indulged in their fantasies and day-dreams and what came through was their desire to stand out from the crowd:

'Like with graffiti, to leave your name, your mark.'

'To be famous and be remembered.'

'I'd like to leave my life's history written on Stonehenge or something like that, so everyone remembers me for ever ... but you haven't got a life's history yet, so who would want to know about you? ... Well I haven't yet ... but I want people to know I was alive.'

'To be someone in the world, not working with machines, putting letters into a machine like my dad ... I want to be doing it for myself.'

'I want to be a footballer, to walk on to the pitch and hear all those people shouting my name.'

'I want to produce something, do something that will be of help for the next people.'

Life after eighteen

But is there life after eighteen? Will they ever have a life history? What will getting older bring? Getting older was too remote for the under fourteens:

'When you're older a lot of people make enemies with you, specially if you've got a lot of money ... like in Dallas, the Ewings have got a lot of money and a lot of enemies.'

'We'll be going to discos and pubs ... I suppose some of

us will get spots ... we might go bald. I'm going to grow a beard and a moustache.'

'Don't know really ... I'll meet more people, have a job, go all over the place and not just stay in one place ... do more things, travel but I'll have more money as I'll be working.'

'I'll be more experienced and be very confident in myself.'

'I hope there's peace and I have a car.'

Me: 'What will you do with your money?'

'Take it on holiday.'

'I just want to be seventeen. It all starts there, you can do anything at seventeen and eighteen.'

'A girl can be engaged, go out wherever she wants, you don't have to stay in or be in bed by 10.30 ... you have a proper boy-friend, go out and drink in a pub.'

'I'll have a house, a car, a family, a good job ... I will have achieved something by the time I'm thirty.'

By fifteen and sixteen it was much more personal ambitions: 'I'll commit suicide when I'm forty, I'd hate to get old ... you see some of those old ladies in the street and I think, "Oh God no, it's horrible." '

'You can still enjoy yourself at forty, if you look youngish, but not if you look like my mum.'

'I want to be different from everyone when I'm forty, when I see my mum get fat and say do your homework all the time it really gets on my nerves ... I'm either going to be different or commit suicide.'

'I won't try and be young again, it's worse when they want to go to discos and everything, middle-aged fat women with a spare tyre and stilettos ... if only they'd try and be themselves and not try and dye their hair bright colours.'

'I couldn't stand it when I stop getting wolf whistles ... because they'll whistle at anybody.'

'One thing I dread doing is ... I'd be so embarrassed ... it's going to collect a pension ... that would really make you feel old.'

'I'm not going to collect a pension because I'll be a famous actress.'

'I can't think that far ahead ... I could be dead in five years.'

'I'm not worried about getting old, I'm just scared of dying.'

Me: 'Will you sniff glue or take drugs when you're older?'

'Oh no.'

Me: 'Why not?'

'You can't get out of your head when you've got about fifteen kids around you ... you've got responsibilities then.'

'... unless you're married to the sort of man who wants his dinner on the table every night when he gets home ... then you need to smoke dope!'

'Don't worry ... I'll be good when I grow up.'

Me: 'But why, if you're naughty now, why stop?'

'What's the point in being naughty. When you're older it's all allowed ... there's nothing to rebel against.'

12 What now?

Some people read this book and feel cheated. 'So what's new?' they say. 'Nothing's changed since I was a teenager.' You can almost hear them begging for the odd titbit of sex and violence. Such people should go straight out and buy a copy of the *News of the World*. This book is not for them. We are not talking about the lunatic fringe, we are talking about teenagers. People love to condemn teenage drinking bouts, shudder at Skinhead violence and purse their lips at Punks in the street. They get a kick out of creating a tribe of aliens. It is more exciting to poke a tiger than a pussy cat. But underneath, they know that *their* sons and daughters, brothers and sisters are not aliens. If they were, the nation would self-destruct.

The kids are not unknown, but they're not the same as their parents either. So what's different? Well, the difference is dramatic if you are living through it and so obvious if you're not, that it's hardly worth mentioning. We'll say it anyway – for the kids THIS IS THE FIRST TIME ROUND.

They are experiencing sensations for the first time – the first love, the first illegal lager, the first holiday away from Mum, the first razor, the first pay packet. This is where the excitement is. They are charged with energy, whether they channel it into playground fights or self-doubt. The emotions are ten times as strong as adults feel.

Grown-ups are used to drinking whisky, spending their own money, choosing where to go on holiday and having sex, but when the kids talk about saving up for a leather jacket, and buying a drink in the pub it may be the first big decision they have ever made. Imagine going up to your boss and informing him that you've decided to implement on your own responsibility the scheme he has just vetoed. This is the magnitude of the decisions we are talking about.

Grown-ups forget what it feels like. They can't help it. When you decide for yourself every night of the week what time to go to bed, it's hard to feel the same as a thirteen-year-old, who stays up to 1.30 a.m. the night his parents go to a dinner-dance. For the kids the pay-off lies in achieving adult privileges, the adult looking back at them sees a thin reflection of himself and dismisses them as boring. Once you're at the top of the mountain, you may lose interest in the path up, but it doesn't mean that the mountain isn't worth climbing.

Adults look to young people to prick their consciences, but that's a lot to expect from teenagers still at school. Their main job is to learn how to be adults first. They can't fight the lions before they even get into the arena. They can't draw a sword until they stop cowering with embarrassment.

At the age of fourteen, it is not what they *say* which is dramatic, it is what they *don't* say. It is what they take for granted which underlines how much things have changed. Of course they still haggle with Mum over clothes and coming-in times, of course they fight with their brothers and sisters, of course they are petrified the first time they go out on a date. But look at the other side. They expect to get instant colour television coverage of a war which breaks out on the other side of the world, they expect to meet violence in school and they expect to decide whether to have sex at the age of fourteen.

The difficult thing about spotting change is that we are all exposed to it. We can all direct-dial New York these days – change isn't only the prerogative of the kids. What's different is that adults see the modern world as the *end* of a long chain of events and kids see it as the beginning. What's new to us is normal to them. They can't see it in perspective.

Nor can they articulate what is wrong with it. They react to what's there. It takes an adult to say 'we expect too much of them', 'they shouldn't be pressured into sex', 'there should be jobs waiting for them, when they leave school'.

Society has diversified with the speed of an atomic chain reaction. The kids cope without thinking about it, but underneath they are begging for structure. They insist that Mum set the limits, that school teachers demand discipline, and that the law of the land be enforced to the letter. They distrust credit cards which would run away with their money and school curricula which offer too much choice. They reject open strife between politicians on the television.

The world is unstable and instability is frightening. The children of divorced parents reject divorce, teenagers who leave school without qualifications are scared. They prize security more than their parents did.

The oldest teenager in this survey was born in 1964. Mum and Dad are in their mid-thirties – children of the sixties. When they left school, everything was possible. They are the first generation to refuse to stop being young. Mum puts on her lipstick and goes out to work, Dad takes his son to listen to The Who concert, sporting long hair and blue jeans. An older generation which clings to its youth is bound to undermine a younger one, because after so much experience, they are naturally better at it. What role does that leave for the younger generation? Are they becoming more conservative or are they coming to tolerate the extremes?

Teenagers who have seen their friend's mum go off with another man, who have been kicked in a football fight, and watched a man being shot dead in a news broadcast, reject all these things with horror. But simply being exposed to them means that they are a familiar part of society and familiarity is the first step towards acceptance. Today's teenagers are more likely than their parents to get divorced, travel abroad and put up with the National Front, for no better reason than that society has got used to the idea.

Children are not required to reflect on the state of the world, their job is to find out how things work at home. Teenagers do have the capacity to reflect, but they don't have the experience to recognize trends. They start with a snapshot of what's around them and add more snapshots as they go along. Eventually they string the snapshots together and end up with a moving picture. Once they see themselves as part of the moving picture, they can decide which direction they want to move in. Until then their values depend on what they have experienced personally. Issues only mean something if they relate back to themselves.

The easiest ideas to grab hold of are the ones which stick out. How sensitive are they to social trends like the Women's Movement? Some people have called the kids sexist because they hang on to traditional sex roles, but if you were taking a first-time snapshot, you'd get a picture of a world where men were dominant too. The kids are still trying to work out what's staring them in the face, value judgements come later.

Sex is at the centre of their lives. Imagine how teenagers feel watching their bodies grow sexy. They define their identities round sex and because they are not yet at ease with the idea, they want to be as unequivocally male or female as they can manage. Boys become aggressive, humorous and hard; girls become pleasing, soft and deferential. This is not sexist in the traditional sense, it is just another example of starting off on the obvious route. It's what they do when they realize where they're going that counts. At sixteen, there are girls going into computers and boys who are learning to cook. The ground work for equality is already laid; a boy expects a girl to pay for her own drink, and a girl expects to go out to work once she's married.

You can't assume that what kids do up to the age of sixteen is going to dog them for the rest of their lives. They expect to move on, and discard the symbols they prized when they were younger. The tragedy comes when they have to make life-long decisions at a time when their thoughts are coloured by a phase they're going to grow out of. Choosing a career, for example – many a good male nurse has been lost that way!

It is the temporary phases which are the meat of teenage culture – fashion, music, violence, drugs. They are visibly different from adult preoccupations because the kids use them to identify themselves as different from adults in the first place.

When they are short of copy, the media love to doomsay about the state of the nation's youth. But it is not at all certain that because they sniff glue today, they will be hooked on heroin in ten years' time. Kids have a strong sense of survival.

And what about the media? The media more than anything have contributed to real change. Kids are bombarded with information, magazines, radio, cinema, advertising and most important of all, television. There are so many sophisticated messages in the air that school looks out of date. 'Tomorrow's World' is riveting, school physics is not. The fantasy future is glittering with Ceefax and videorecorders and videophones. The concepts generated by technology become part of everyday life. 'Action replay' bawled Andy, when I got something wrong in the group. His father could never have chosen that expression. The media drum home the variety, it raises awareness, and creates expectations. It multiplies a hundredfold the teenagers' knowledge of how other people live, and it helps them to spread the youth culture. It opens the door to adventure but it offers no way to walk through it. Today's media are one-way. The kids can dive through a school of sharks with Jacques Cousteau, and answer questions in the House, alongside Margaret Thatcher, but they can't make their opinions known outside their own front door. There is no channel of communication for them. When they can't communicate, they are hurt, they become disaffected 'It's all a con, why should I bother anyway?'

Some of them demand recognition through violence. The Skinhead whose photograph adorns the front cover of the colour supplement has broken through. Others just get frustrated, they don't see what place the nation intends for them. It's cosy being a teenager – as long as you wear the right clothes and like the right music, you belong. But where are they meant to go afterwards?

Kids hate being forced to think ahead, it's hard enough to work out patterns from the past, let alone the future. They are scared because they can't imagine what it will be like.

Society is sending out messages full of double meanings; 'We need more women engineers.' 'It's Mum's job to look after the children.' 'Save your money for a rainy day.' 'This time next year a loaf of bread will cost twice as much.' 'You can't wear a mini skirt.' 'Cor, look at page three!' 'Young people have more opportunities than ever before.' 'There isn't a job for you.'

The kids have never known it any other way. They are not complaining. They are not optimistic either. They know they have to go out and hustle, things won't be handed to them on a plate. There is a grimness about them. Pop songs often touch a nerve – consider the words of this song which reached the Hit Parade in 1980:

You've got to be a hustler, if you want to get on
Principles will only hold you back
Everyone who's making it
Is getting out and shaking it.

They are hardening up for an increasingly hard world.

Selected Bestsellers

☐	**The Amityville Horror**	Jay Anson	80p
☐	**The Health Food Guide**	Michael Balfour and Ruby Rae	£1.50p
☐	**The Island**	Peter Benchley	£1.25p
☐	**Smart-Aleck Kill**	Raymond Chandler	95p
☐	**The Entity**	Frank De Felitta	£1.25p
☐	**Whip Hand**	Dick Francis	£1.50p
☐	**Solo**	Jack Higgins	£1.50p
☐	**The Rich are Different**	Susan Howatch	£1.95p
☐	**Moviola**	Garson Kanin	£1.50p
☐	**The Empty Copper Sea**	John D. MacDonald	90p
☐	**Where There's Smoke**	Ed McBain	80p
☐	**Spike Island**	James McClure	£1.95p
☐	**The Master Mariner Book 1: Running Proud**	Nicholas Monsarrat	£1.50p
☐	**Bad Blood**	Richard Neville and Julie Clarke	£1.50p
☐	**The Queen and Lord M**	Jean Plaidy	£1.50p
☐	**Fools Die**	Mario Puzo	£1.50p
☐	**Sunflower**	Marilyn Sharp	95p
☐	**The Throwback**	Tom Sharpe	95p
☐	**Wild Justice**	Wilbur Smith	£1.50p
☐	**That Old Gang of Mine**	Leslie Thomas	£1.25p
☐	**Caldo Largo**	Earl Thompson	£1.50p
☐	**Harvest of the Sun**	E. V. Thompson	£1.25p
☐	**The Third Wave**	Alvin Toffler	£1.95p

All these books are available at your local bookshop or newsagent, or can be ordered direct from the publisher. Indicate the number of copies required and fill in the form below

Name_____

(block letters please)

Address_____

_____

Send to Pan Books (CS Department), Cavaye Place, London SW10 9PG
Please enclose remittance to the value of the cover price plus:

25p for the first book plus 10p per copy for each additional book ordered
to a maximum charge of £1.05 to cover postage and packing
Applicable only in the UK

While every effort is made to keep prices low, it is sometimes
necessary to increase prices at short notice. Pan Books reserve
the right to show on covers and charge new retail prices which
may differ from those advertised in the text or elsewhere